Google Forms in the Classroom

Second Edition

By Kathe L. Santillo, M. Ed.

All efforts have been made to ensure this book is accurate at the time of publishing. Information in this book is based on the version of all software applications at the time of publishing and may not reflect changes in the software after that time.

About the Author

Kathe L. Santillo is a library media specialist at the Butler Area Senior High School in Butler, Pennsylvania. She earned a Bachelor of Science in Education (Library Science, k-12) from Slippery Rock University in 1995; and a Master of Education from Mansfield University (Mansfield, PA) with specialization in school library and information technologies, in 2002.

Kathe served as an Instructional Technology Coach for the Butler Area School District from 2006 to 2011. She was selected as a Pennsylvania District Level and State Level *Keystone Technology Integrator* for excellence in integrating technology into the curriculum in 2005. Kathe was born and raised in Columbus, Ohio and attended Columbus South High School and The Ohio State University before moving to Pennsylvania.

Table of Contents

Chapter 1: Introduction to Google Forms

What is Google Forms?

Google Forms is one of the available applications in *Google Drive*, Google's cloud-based file storage, creation, and collaboration tool. Unlike documents and spreadsheets created in Microsoft Word, or other traditional software applications, you can create and access any documents, Forms or spreadsheets you create in *Google Drive* anywhere you can access the Web, including smart phones and tablets. This book is based on the *free* public version of Google Forms. If you are using Google for Education apps, some settings may be slightly different.

Google Forms is a very useful tool that can be used in a variety of ways, especially in the classroom. Google Forms enables you to create an electronic Form for gathering multiple types of data. If you think about it, almost any traditional assessment tool you create and use with your students does the exact same thing - it collects data in the Form of answers, summaries, reflections, and facts. The Form itself lets you create data entry fields for several types of data input, such as multiple choice, short text, paragraph text, checkboxes, choose from a list, scale, and grid. When you create your Form, You also create a destination spreadsheet which is also added to your Google Drive files. Once students complete a Form and submit it, their responses can automatically feed into the destination spreadsheet, or another spreadsheet designated by you. Google Forms can be used across all levels of learning - from simple recall and comprehension to evaluation, reflection, and debate.

Each Form completed by you is assigned a unique URL address, enabling students to access it and complete it online. Google Forms can be shared through email or links; or can be embedded in Web pages. When the students are done entering their data, they click SUBMIT at the bottom of the Form, and the data comes to you in one document, accessible anywhere online, making assessment easier.

Google Forms can be used for classroom management, Formative and summative assessment, reading logs, sign-up sheets, and everything in between! They are simple to create, but can be extremely powerful assessment tools. Using GF in the classroom, a teacher (or even students) can create, collate, and process data easily and effectively.

This book will walk you step-by-step through all of the processes of using Google Forms in the classroom - setting up a Google account, creating and customizing multiple types of Forms, and Formatting and evaluating data. You will learn how to use Google Forms to: create branching lessons and quizzes for differentiated instruction; how to add multimedia to use Forms as writing prompts to encourage critical thinking; how to create self-grading quizzes; how to Format spreadsheet cells so that the gathered data is easier to assess; and much, much more. Below are some example uses for Google Forms in the classroom.

1.1 - Uses for Google Forms in the Classroom

CLASSROOM MANAGEMENT & DAY-TO-DAY ACTIVITIES	LESSONS, ASSESSMENT & REFLECTION
Sign-up Sheets	Interest Surveys
Class Information Management	Learner Self-Monitoring Reports
Nomination Forms	Reading Journals
Make-up Request Form for Parents	Learning Logs
Teacher/Colleague Observation	Quizzes & Tests
Attendance Check-ins	Writing Prompts
Annotated Bibliography Collection	Observation Rubrics
Assignment Submitting (Link)	Instant Feedback on Lessons or Instruction
Snack Sign-up Forms	Student-to-Student Data Collection Projects
Scheduling Parent-Teacher Conference	Data Collection for Experiments
Volunteer Sign-up	Peer Feedback
Department & School-wide Surveys	K-W-L for Assessing Prior Knowledge
Technology Issues Reporting Tool	Reading Record
Getting to Know You Class Survey	Project Progress Form
Dialoging with Parents	Observation Tools (checklists; anecdotal notes, etc.)
Placing Orders for Fundraisers	Questioning
Parental Feedback	Beginning-of-Year Technology Skills Survey
Discipline Referrals	Student-Created Choose Your Own Adventure Stories
Creating Lesson Plans	Debate Social Attitudes Form
Manage Classroom Lending Libraries	Website Evaluation Form
Parental Absence Notice	Student Note-Taking
Topic Sign-up Sheets	Global Collaboration
Computer Lab Reservation Form	Exit Tickets
Grading/Observation Rubric	Reservations for Class Trips

As mentioned earlier, this book also covers different types of assessment tools that can be created and utilized through Google Forms. A note, however - if you are looking for a book that will guide you through the theory of formative and summative assessment, this is not the book for you. This book *will* discuss the characteristics of different types of assessments to create in Google Forms, but was primarily written to guide you through creating each assessment, instructional, or management tool, as well as assessing and sharing the data quickly and effectively. That way, you can get to the real business of the classroom - meeting and addressing the instructional needs of your students.

Why Should You Use Google Forms in the Classroom?

As evident in the examples listed in *Table 1.1,* there are many ways to use Google Forms in the classroom. No matter which way you choose to use the Forms, the benefits are the same:

    1. The Forms are readily available to you wherever you have an Internet connection.

    2. The Forms can easily be used with different devices: handhelds, such as iPod Touch © or smart phones; laptops; tablets; or desktop computers. They are supported by both Android and IOS devices.

    3. The Forms streamline your results and make your data manageable.

    4. Data and Forms can be easily shared with others.

    5. The Forms can be re-used and modified as your needs change.

    6. Forms can provide instant feedback, which can be used formatively, or shared as part of a lesson introduction.

Google Forms let you collect large amounts of data which is streamlined to one place. The instant feedback from assessments or lessons allow data-driven decisions to be made in real-time during instruction. This means you have the opportunity to identify and remediate; have open dialog or on-demand Q and A; group and differentiate instruction by color coding responses with conditional formatting; have students demonstrate reasoning using specific question types (*paragraph, linear scale*) or demonstrate sequencing (using *dropdown* across multiple questions).

Using Google Forms enables embedding formative assessment so that it flows naturally with class instruction, without interruptions in the instruction.

Results from large data collection can be graphed and shared with other project stakeholders. The possibilities for using Google Forms in the classroom are endless!

Integrating and Assessing Thinking Skills...

Google Forms offers a wide variety of question types and data field choices. Because of these choices, if you create quizzes and tests, they do not have to be limited to simple yes/no, true/false, or multiple choice questions. You can include data field choices that enable the student to input well-thought out text responses to evoke higher order thinking skills.

With a little extra work, you can also set up a Google Form so that the data (answers/responses) submitted by the student feed automatically into a pre-formatted document (using *Save as Doc* or *Autocrat* add-ons). These documents are held in a designated assignment folder, and can be graded and handed back to the student, or shared with other teachers or administrators. *Autocrat* can also be used to generate and send certificates and awards from information entered into a Form.

Because Google Forms is Web-based and therefore, *mobile*, a tablet, iPod Touch ®, or smart phone can be used as you observe students working, enabling on-demand Formative assessment. As with all uses of Google Forms, the data from those observations can be streamlined into one location for thorough review later, and can be shared in print or electronically with colleagues and administrators.

Chapter 2: The Basics

Getting Started with Google Forms

There are a few housekeeping tasks you will need to do in order to make your use of Google Forms possible and efficient.
1. Create a Google Account.
2. Add a Google Drive shortcut to your computer desktop OR install the Google Drive app.
3. Add the Google Drive app to any tablets or smart phones you plan to use for instructional or assessment purposes.
4. Install and use the Google Chrome operating system on the computers or handheld devices you will use with your Forms.

The first option from the list above is necessary in order to use Google Forms. The other three are optional, but will make your use of Google Forms more efficient.

1. Creating a Google Account

Creating a Google account will enable you to access to all of Google's services, including Google Mail (Gmail) and Google Drive. Google Drive is a two-fold service. First, it serves as a place to store your document files and other files in the cloud so they can be accessed anywhere you have an Internet connection. Documents created in *Word* or Adobe PDF documents can also be uploaded and stored in Google Drive folders. Secondly, Google Drive offers a suite of software applications that you can use to create, edit, and collaboratively share documents with others. This application suite includes several tools similar to the older versions (circa 2003) of Microsoft Word (word processing), Excel (spreadsheet), and PowerPoint (presentation).

The Google Forms tool is also included in the application suite, but differs from any Microsoft tool, so some users shy away from it because it is not a familiar tool. However, Google Forms is an easy-to-use, powerful and versatile tool, especially for educators.

To Create Your Free Google Account:

Go to the Google homepage at http://www.google.com. A "Sign In" link will be visible in the upper-right corner of the Google homepage. If you do not have a Google account, you must create one. You will need to enter a username, which will also be your Google Mail address; a password; your date of birth (for age verification); your gender; a mobile phone number, in case you lose your password; and a verification email address. Since the usernames must be unique, if the one you chose is already in use, Google will suggest an alternative. You can also opt to *not* create a Gmail account, by selecting the link underneath of the username field to create your Google account with an existing email address. Once you've completed the CAPTCHA, which lets Google know that you are a real person, you must agree with the privacy policy and Terms of Service before clicking the "Next Step" button. Next, Google takes you to your profile page. You can choose to add a picture at this time, or add one later (or not at all). Click the "Get Started" button, and your Google account is created! Your Google account is now usable in any of the Google services, including Google Drive.

2. Add a Desktop Shortcut to Google Drive

If your computer or tablet operating system does not automatically create a desktop shortcut, you will want to add one for quick access to your files and Google Drive services. Please refer to your operating system manual or the help section of your operating system for instructions on how to create a desktop shortcut.   **OR**

3. Install the Google Drive App on Mobile Devices

Even if you do not plan to use your Forms on a mobile device in the classroom, there are many reasons why you would want the Google Drive app on your phone and/or tablet. These reasons will be covered later in this book, but having the app on your smart phone and/or tablet comes in very handy!

4. Install the Google Chrome Browser

What's the best reason for installing Google Chrome? It's awesome!! What's the best reason for installing Google Chrome when using Google Drive services? Bonus features! The Google Chrome Web store has many "plugin" extensions and add-on apps, which, when downloaded, enhance the Google Chrome and Google Drive services with added bonus features. For example, if you install Google Chrome as your Internet browser then go to the Chrome Web store and download the Google Drive app, you will have *automatic* offline access to your Google Drive documents and automatic syncing. Another Chrome app lets you save Web content and screen captures directly to Google Drive.

Understanding the Basics of *Google Drive*

A working knowledge of Google Drive is necessary to use the Google Forms application. Google Drive is itself a very powerful and feature-packed tool. It would take a whole other book (or at least a lot more pages to this one) to cover all of the details of

Google Drive, so this book will only cover what a user needs to know to use Google Forms in a variety of ways so he/she can complete the instructional, assessment, and managerial tools needed.

To use Google Drive, either download and install the Google Drive application to a computer, or access it exclusively through a Web browser. If a user chooses to download and install the app, there are some extra features available, such as automatic syncing of documents on the user's computer to the Google Drive cloud storage. Users choose to install the Google Chrome browser as well, since there are several downloadable extensions (enhancements) and features that integrate with the Google Drive.

Accessing Google Drive through the Web Browser

Google Drive can be accessed from the main Google homepage. Go to http://www.google.com and sign in to your Google account by clicking on "Sign In" in the upper-right corner. Once signed in, click on the Apps icon in the upper-right corner, as shown below.

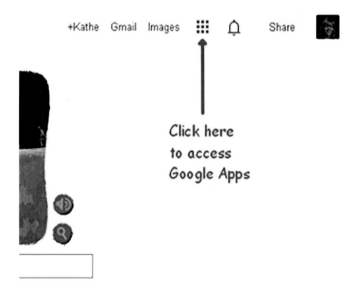

The first time a user logs in to Google Drive, it will look a little bare. Don't worry, once you start creating Forms, it won't continue to look that way! Below is an image showing what Google Drive looks like the first time a user logs in.

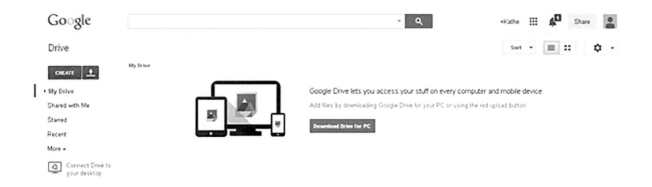

The Google Drive Environment (first time access)

Once you start creating Forms, the center area will be populated with the documents (Forms and destination spreadsheets) that were created, and it will look like this:

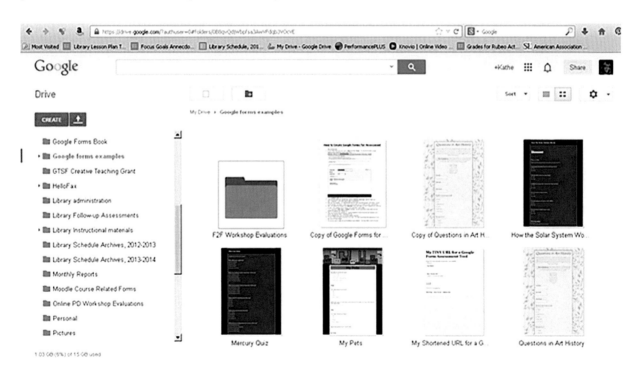

Now that a Google Drive account is created, you can start creating Google Forms.

Understanding the Basics of Google Forms

When a Google Form is created, you are actually creating three different documents at one time. **A Google Form consists of three different, but linked, parts**. They are: the *editing template*, the *live Form*, and the *destination spreadsheet*.

Editing Template

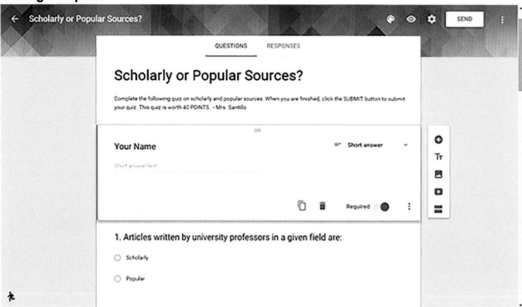

The *editing template* is the "guts" of a Google Form. It is where you enter questions and information through the selection of different types of data fields. It is where the creating process takes place. Any future editing to a Form is also done through the editing template.

Live Form

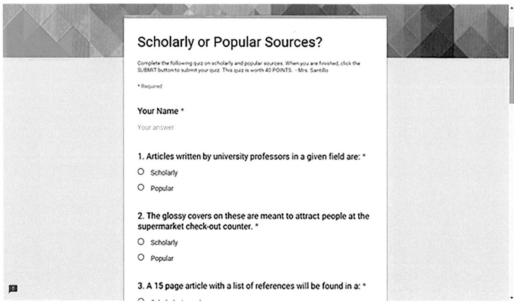

The *live Form* is what students, parents, administrators, or any participants will see. Each live Form is assigned a unique link so that it can be accessed by the people asked to complete it. Any questions, information, images, videos, etc. that are placed in the editing template will be visible in the live Form. The live Form can also be accessed and completed on mobile devices, such as smart phones and tablets. It can be printed, completed by hand, and turned in by students in paper format.

Destination Spreadsheet

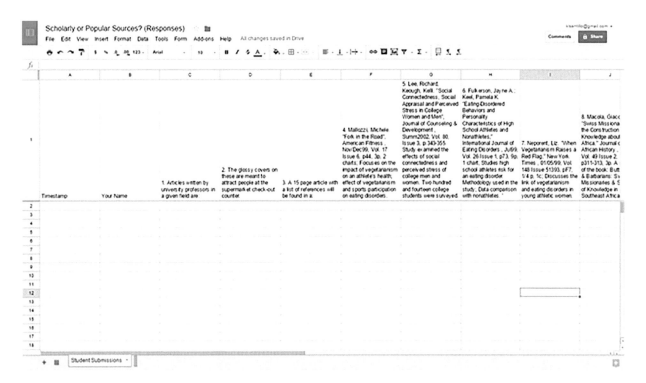

The *destination spreadsheet* is where all of the responses are collected once the live Form is completed and submitted. The Form creator can elect to create a new spreadsheet each time he/she creates a new Form, or have the results sent to an existing spreadsheet.

Destination spreadsheet options and features will be covered in more detail throughout this book.

Chapter 3: Creating the Form

Okay, now that you are the proud owner of a Google Drive account, let's start making Google Forms.

Sign in to your Google Drive account. When the Google Drive environment appears, click on the red *NEW* button. Next, select *MORE* from the list of options, then select *GOOGLE FORMS.*

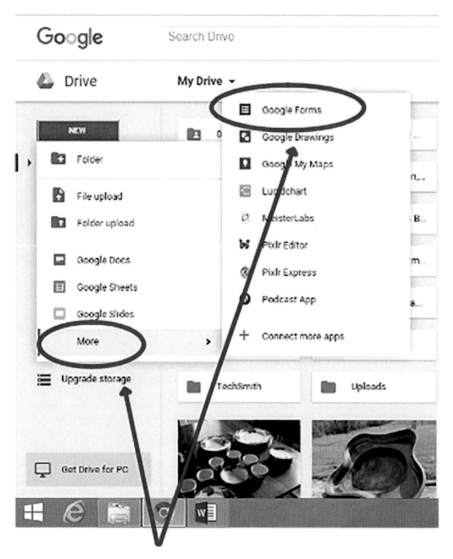

Select MORE, then select
GOOGLE FORMS

The editing template for the Form will open. This is where the student instructions, questions, reading prompts, choices, images, videos, etc. are added to each Google Form created.

THE EDITING TEMPLATE

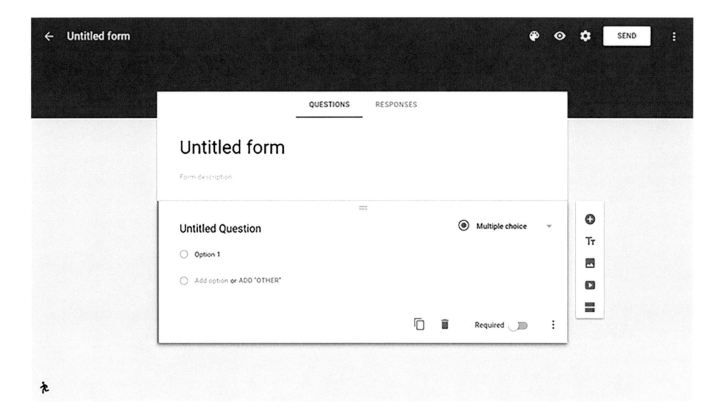

The Editing Template Explained

The Editing Template – Questions Tab

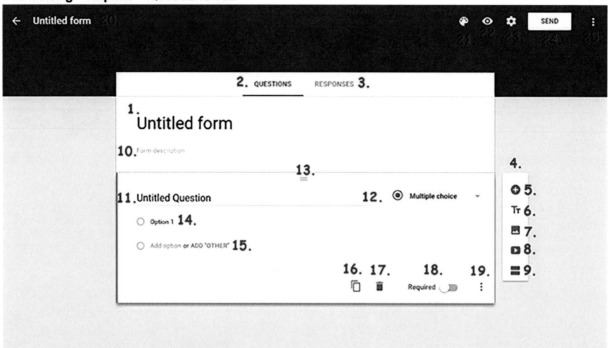

The Editing Template – Responses Tab

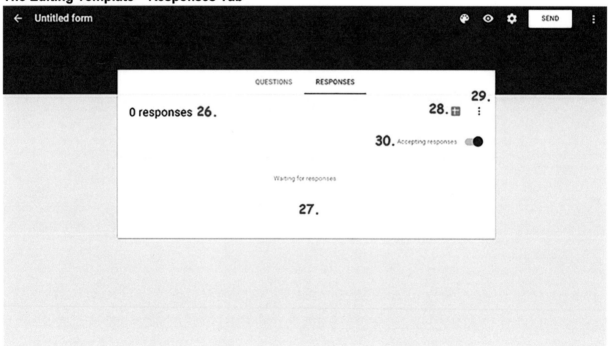

Here's a general overview of the editing template. Each area's use will be discussed in detail later. The editing template will change based on certain question types used in the Form. These will be explained when the specific question types are discussed later in the book.

1. Form Title – This area will include the title given to the Form.

2. Questions Tab – This is the default tab the editing template opens to display.

3. Responses Tab – This tab is selected to toggle to the Responses settings.

4. Editing Toolbar – Several editing functions are available through this toolbar menu.

5. Add Question – Select this to add another question to the Form. Depending on the question type picked, a *conditional branching* option can be selected from the question type area. This lets the Form creator direct users to different questions, depending on the responses given.

6. Add Heading & Description – Works like a sub-heading. Enables breaking a Form into chunks. Each "chunk" can then be labeled with a heading, and a description can be added for instructions, etc.

7. Add Image – Select this to add an image to the Form.

8. Add Video – Select this to link to and add a YouTube video to the Form.

9. Add Section – Select this to break a Form into sections. Each section is displayed on its own page.

10. Form Description – Information or instructions to be displayed for the users.

11. Question Title – Text area where the question or a displayed label (ex. *First Name, Last Name,* etc.) is added. This will cue users as to what data is to be added in the open text box field.

12. Question Type – There are eleven different question types to choose from: *short answer, paragraph, multiple choice, checkboxes, dropdown, file upload, linear scale, multiple choice grid, checkbox grid, date,* and *time.*

13. Drag and Drop – Hover the mouse over this area to move a question up or down in the Form.

14. Choice Option(s) – Area where answers or choices are listed.

15. Add "Other" – Inserts a text field labeled, *Other* and includes a textbox for the student-entered option.

16. Duplicate Question – Duplicates the question.

17. Delete Question – Deletes the question.

18. Required Question Toggle – Requires the user to complete the question before the Form can be submitted. This should ALWAYS be ON for a name or other identifier field. This can be set as a default setting in Forms so that every question entered on any Form is required. BE CAREFUL using this as the default, though. There are circumstances where you may not require every field to have data in it, and setting this by default will require the respondents to enter data in that field.

19. Additional Question Settings - Use this area to display *help text,* which provides an explanation or more detailed instructions for the user (ex. *Select the best match from* *the list below)*; to shuffle the order of answer options; or to *branch* a question (send a respondent to a different question B, based on the response to question A).

20. Form Title Display – Click this area to add or edit a title (or file name) for the Form.

21. Color Palette – Change the theme color of the Form, or choose from a library of illustrated backgrounds.

22. Preview – Enables viewing the Form in its "live" mode. This is how a respondent will see the Form when it is completed.

23. Settings - Clicking on *Settings* opens a dialog box where changes can be made to Form settings. The *Settings* area is divided into three areas. They are: ***General, Presentation,*** and ***Quizzes***. Each area has its own settings. The *General* settings are default settings for ALL Forms created.

The options under the ***General*** settings tab are:

Collect email addresses – This option collects the email addresses of respondents who submit a completed Form.

Response Receipts – If *collect email addresses* is activated, the Form creator can enable this feature and all respondents will receive a copy of their responses.

Limit to One Response – If this setting is selected, respondents must be signed in to a Google account.

Respondents Can Edit After Submit – This enables respondents to change their answers after they've submitted them.

Respondents Can See Summary Charts and Text Responses – Enables respondents to see a summary of everyone's responses.

***Presentation Settings*:**

Confirmation Page Message – Create a unique message here that students will see after they complete the Form and click the SUBMIT button to send the completed Form.

Show Link to Submit Another Response – Displays the link to the Form on the confirmation page which allows respondents to submit another response.

Show Progress Bar – Add a progress bar to be displayed on longer Forms which have been divided into sections using the *add section* option. The progress bar displays the percentage of the Form that was completed on each section page.

Shuffle Question Order - shuffle the display of the question order.

Quizzes Settings:

Make This a Quiz – Selecting this toggle option assigns a point value to each question and enables auto-grading.

Release Grade – If a Form is designated a quiz, the Form creator can select between *immediately after each submission* or *later, after manual review*. Selecting the "later" option turns on the email collection feature of the Form.

Respondent Can See Missed Questions – Selecting this enables respondents to immediately see the results of the quiz. Each missed question is highlighted, and the correct answer is displayed.

24. Send Button – Enables how respondents access the Form. The options are email the Form; provide a link to the Form; or embed the Form in a Web page using a provided embed code.

25. More Settings - This menu provides additional options for your Form. These include an *undo* option; making a copy of the Form; moving it to the trash; getting a pre-filled link; printing; adding collaborators; using a script editor; get add-ons; preferences, which adds default settings to all Forms. These settings include collecting email addresses of submitted Forms; making all questions required; and setting a default point value for quiz questions. The option for *Get Pre-Filled Link* enables the creation of a copy of a Form with specified fields already filled in with data or information. The *Print* option will print a paper version of the Form that can also be completed by students and handed in.

Tools under the *Responses Tab*

26. Responses Submitted – Displays the current number of responses submitted to the Form. Once responses begin to populate the destination spreadsheet, buttons appear to view responses as a summary or individually.

27. Summary of Responses Area – Once responses begin to populate the destination spreadsheet, a graphic representation of the data is displayed in this area. Textual responses (*short answer, paragraph*) are displayed as textual entries, while all other question types are displayed in graphic format, such as a pie chart.

28. Create/View Responses – This icon is used first to create the destination spreadsheet. Once created, clicking on the icon enables viewing of the destination spreadsheet and the responses.

29. Responses Setting Menu – The options here are to *Get Email Notification for New Responses; Select Response Destination; Unlink Form; Download Responses (.csv); Print All Responses* and *Delete All Responses.*

30. Accepting Responses Toggle – This can be toggled to turn response acceptance on or off.

Adding Questions and Instructions to the Form Editing Template

The Form editing template is where you begin building your Form.

The *Form description area* appears just below the Form title. This is a great place to put any details or instructions students should know before they start the Form. It's a good idea to include how the students are to turn in this Form, i.e. "Please click the *Submit* button".

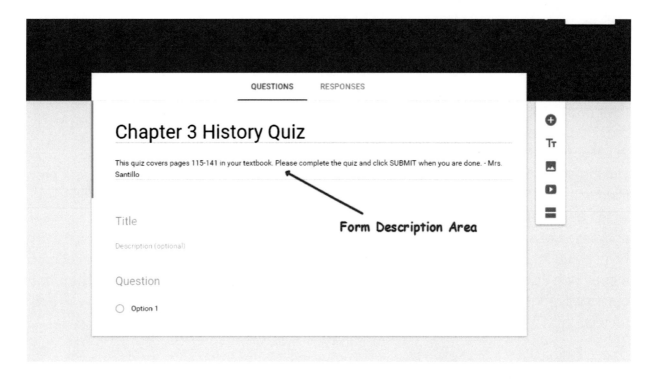

Form Description Area

Once the Form description is completed you can start adding your questions/fields. The editing template is pre-populated with one question area. To begin editing this area, click on the *question field*.

Click on the *Question Editing Area* to begin editing the question.

Question Editing Area

The Question Editing Area

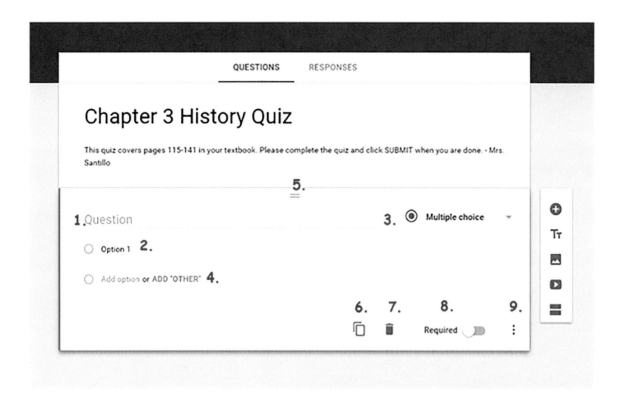

The question editing area is where each question is created or edited, beginning with the **Question Title (1)**. This label, *Question Title*, is sort of misleading, and tends to confuse some people. The Question Title is actually the question, statement, or field label itself. For instance, if you planned to ask a question, such as, "*Who was the first president of the United States?*" you would type that question in the Question Title textbox. If you want the student's last name to be the first area for student input on the Form, you would type *Last Name* in the Question Title textbox. If you wanted to type a scenario as a reading prompt, it would be typed in the Question Title textbox. Whatever it is that the students will be responding to – goes in the Question Title textbox. I personally prefer to use the first few question areas for the student first and last names and the date. If the first and last names are in separate fields as opposed to being together in one field, then the responses in the spreadsheet can be sorted by last name and make reviewing and assessing a little easier.

In the example below, the question title *Last Name* was entered in the textbox. Since students don't need multiple choices to pick their last names, we need to change the **Question Type (3)** to reflect the type of data students will be entering.

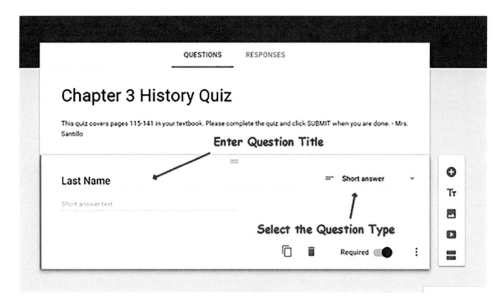

Question Types in Google Forms

There are eleven **question types** in Google Forms. They are: ***short answer, paragraph, multiple choice, checkboxes, dropdown, file upload, linear scale, multiple choice grid, checkbox grid, date***, and ***time***. Each question type has the option to make a response required by clicking the *required toggle button,* so you will need to consider whether or not the questions you add MUST have data entered in the field before the submission will be accepted. It's advisable to make student information, such as first name, last name, class period, grade, etc., required so that no anonymous submissions will be received.

Here is a brief description of the question types:

Short Answer – Works well for short, written text responses. Ex. – *First Name; last name; Short sentences; short phrases; spelling tests.*

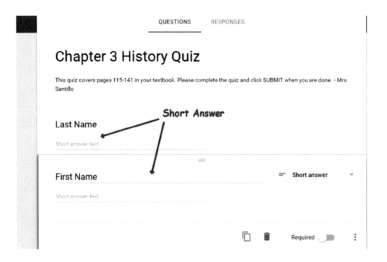

Paragraph – This question type works well for longer, written text responses. Ex. – *Essay responses; responses to writing prompts; summaries.*

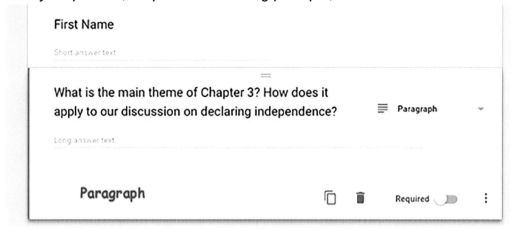

Multiple Choice – Respondents pick **one option** from choices, or add an option using the "*other*" field. Multiple choice question type can also be used to create true/false responses by labeling one choice *true* and one choice *false.*

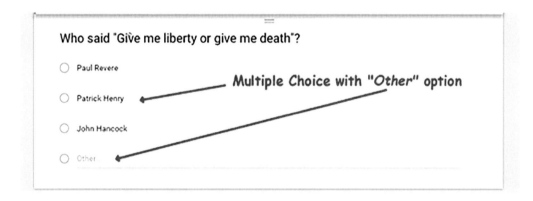

Checkboxes - This question type lets respondents pick as **many options** as they'd like, in other words, when there may be more than one answer. An example of the use of this question type would be any question where students "*choose all that apply*".

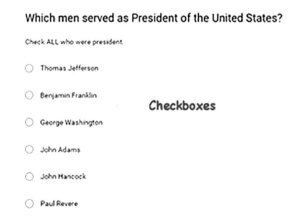

Dropdown - This question type lets the respondent select **one option** from a drop-down menu list. This question type works well when there is a long list of choice options. This question type also works well for sequencing.

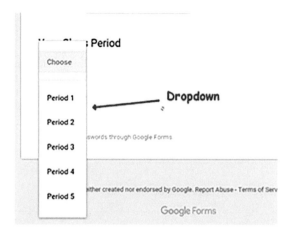

File Upload – This question type lets the respondent submit a single file or multiple files through the Form. Submitted files are then stored in a Google Drive folder under the Form creator's Google Drive account. This is ideal for submission of permission slips and student homework.

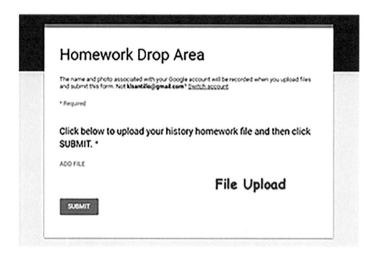

Linear Scale – This question type lets the respondent rank something along a designated scale of numbers. Scales are good to use for rubrics, peer and general evaluations. The highest number on the scale rating question type is 10.

Linear Scale

Was this lesson clearly explained and easy to understand?

	1	2	3	4	5	6	7	
No, it was not explained well	O	O	O	O	O	O	O	Yes, it was explained very well

25

Multiple Choice Grid – This question type works as a grid scale for rating or as a multiple choice matching grid for more than one question. It takes up less space on a Form than placing a scale or multiple choice question type for each question. See the examples below:

Multiple Choice Grid - Matching Example

Match the correct colors

	Verde	Azul	Amarillo	Negro	Rojo
Yellow	O	O	O	O	O
Black	O	O	O	O	O
Green	O	O	O	O	O
Red	O	O	O	O	O
Blue	O	O	O	O	O

Multiple Choice Grid - As a matching question

Multiple Choice Grid – Rating Tool

Rate the Speaker

	1	2	3	4	5
Speaks clearly	O	O	O	O	O
Makes eye contact	O	O	O	O	O
Speaks confidently	O	O	O	O	O
Uses diverse vocabulary	O	O	O	O	O
Maintains audience attention	O	O	O	O	O

Multiple Choice Grid - As a rating tool

26

Checkbox Grid – If a respondent needs to be able to select multiple choices, then the Checkbox Grid question type should be used. The Checkbox Grid is presented in a grid of columns and rows.

Date – This question type inserts a date field which includes a drop-down calendar for quick date selection. There is also an option to add a *time field* with the date field. The time field includes hour, minute, and AM/PM selection. Even without the time field, all submissions are time-stamped so you can track when an assignment (Form) is submitted without adding the time field here.

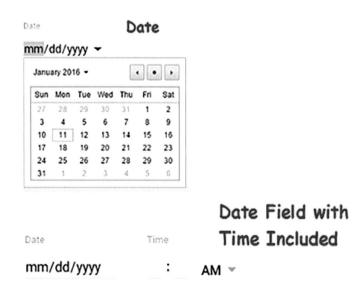

Time – The *time* question type can be used a couple of ways. It can be used to insert a field where respondents can enter the time they begin and finish a projector, such as an activity log; or it can be used to enter the time they begin a quiz or assignment. If you want to use the time question type to determine the duration it takes to complete the Form quiz or assignment, it is not necessary to place a time question type at the beginning *and* end of the Form. Once a respondent submits the completed Form, it will be time-stamped with the submittal time, so simply inserting a time field at the beginning of the Form will inevitably give *both* the start and finish time for the Form completion.

Hrs Min Sec

: :

Time, Duration Checked

Time

: AM

Time, NO Duration Checked

How to Add Each Question Type

Let's take a look at how to add each type of question field. To add additional question types to the Form, first make sure the *Questions Tab* is active, then click on the *Add Question Button* in the *editing toolbar* and select the question type from the drop-down menu in the *question editing area*. You can change the question type after it is created if another type is desired by clicking on the question and selecting a different type.

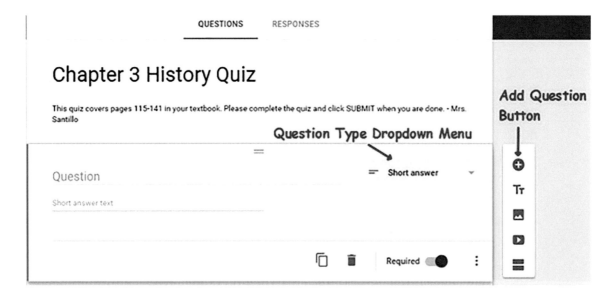

Short Answer Question Type

The *short answer* field works best for data that consists of a few words. Although there is no character limit on this field, the text area is smaller and students will not be able to view a longer text entry, such as an answer to an essay question, in order to make corrections to spelling, etc. To add a *short answer* question type, simple select it from the question type drop-down menu.

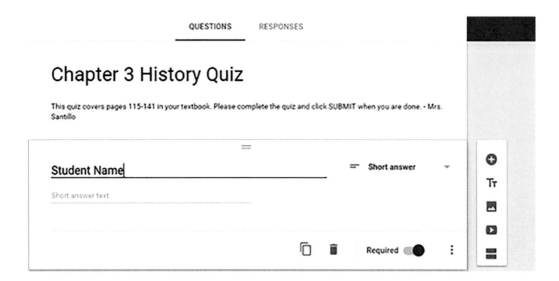

Paragraph Question Type

This is the "field of choice" for longer responses, such as answers to essay questions or any answer or data entry that requires more than a few words. The response text area is bigger than the *text* question type so students can monitor what they are typing. To add a *paragraph* question type, simple select *paragraph* from the question type drop-down.

A maximum or minimum character count can be set on *paragraph* question types by selecting the vertical dots in the bottom or the question area and selecting *data validation.*

Paragraph Question with Data Validation Selected

Multiple Choice Question Type

Select the *multiple choice* question type from the drop-down menu. The question editing area will display one choice option. To add additional answer choice options, click below the previous option and another answer option field will appear or hit the *Enter* key on the keyboard to advance to the next answer option. *Multiple choice* question types include a *branching option,* labeled "go to page based on answer". This feature, which will be covered in detail in a later section, enables you to differentiate instruction by directing the students to a different follow-up question based on the response they give to a branched question. The *multiple choice* question type also has an additional answer option for "other". To add an "other" option field, click on the *Add "Other"* linked text below the options list. Doing this adds a text field for students to input their own text response. Answer options can be re-ordered by dragging the two horizontal lines to the left of each option field. Answer options can be deleted by clicking on the X to the right of each answer option.

Moving or Deleting an Answer Option

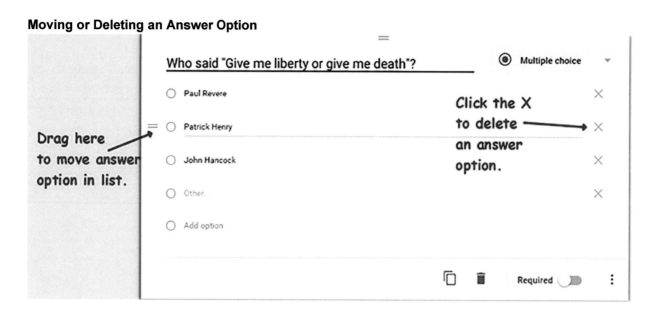

Who said "Give me liberty or give me death"?   ◉ Multiple choice   ▼

○ Paul Revere   ✕

○ Patrick Henry   ✕

Drag here
to move answer
option in list.

○ John Hancock   ✕

Click the X
to delete → ✕
an answer
option.

○ Other   ✕

○ Add option

[copy icon] [trash icon]   Required ⬤   ⋮

Adding a Branching Option

Who said "Give me liberty or give me death"?   ◉ Multiple choice   ▼   ⊕

                                                                                Tᴛ

○ Paul Revere   ✕   🖾

○ Patrick Henry   ✕   ▶

○ John Hancock   ✕   ☰

Click *Additional Question Settings*
to add hint text, branch a question,
or shuffle the order appearance of
the answer options.

○ Other   ✕

○ Add option

[copy icon] [trash icon]   Required

Show

Hint text

Go to section based on answer

Shuffle option order

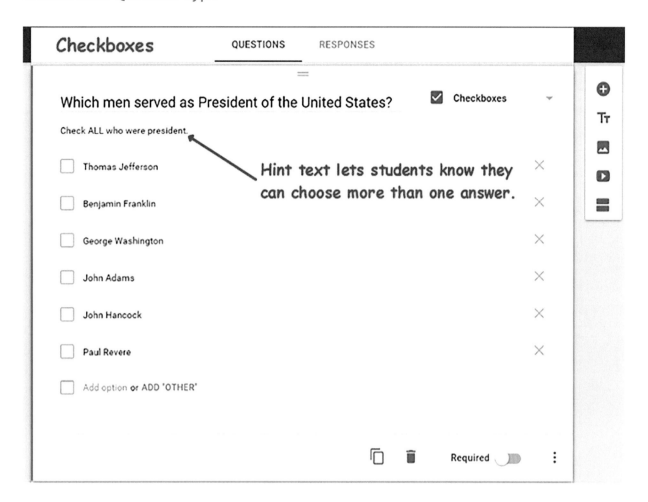

Select the *checkboxes* question type from the question type drop-down menu in the question editing area. To add additional answer choice options, click below the previous option and another answer option field will appear or hit the *Enter* key on the keyboard to advance to the next answer option. It is a good idea to use the *help text* area when including a *checkboxes* question type so that students are aware they may select more than one answer. The other features of this question type, such as the drag and drop, delete, and "other" options, function like their option counterparts in the multiple choice question type.

Dropdown Question Type

This option was known as the "choose from a list" question type in earlier versions of Google Forms. Select the *dropdown* question type from the drop-down in the question editing area when adding a new item. To add additional answer choice options, click below the previous option and another answer option field will appear or hit the *Enter* key on the keyboard to advance to the next answer option. The *dropdown* question type also has a *branching option,* like the multiple choice question type, to enable differentiated learning.

Dropdown question types are good to use when there are many possible answer options, because the option list does not take up a lot of room in the Form area.

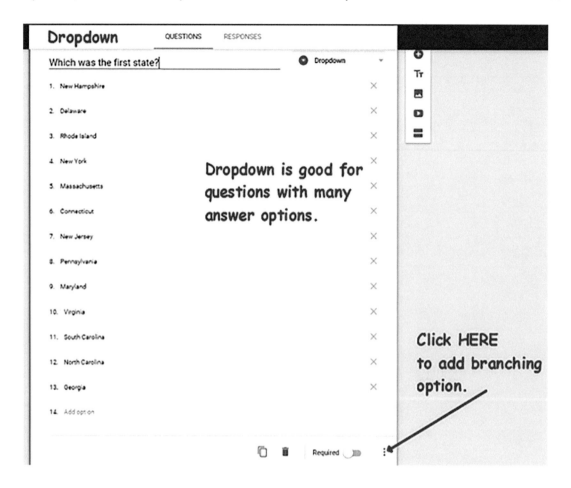

The Dropdown Question in the Live Form

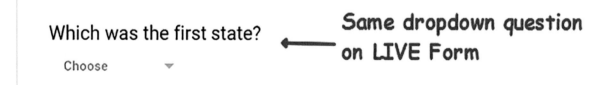

File Upload Question Type

The *file upload* question type enables students, parents, volunteers, etc. to attach and submit a file using the Google Form. Respondents are required to sign in using a Google account FIRST, so it is a good idea to let students, parents, etc., know this prior to using a Google Form with the *file upload* question added in case they does not have a Google account. There is a reminder about this that appears when the *file upload* question type is selected each time.

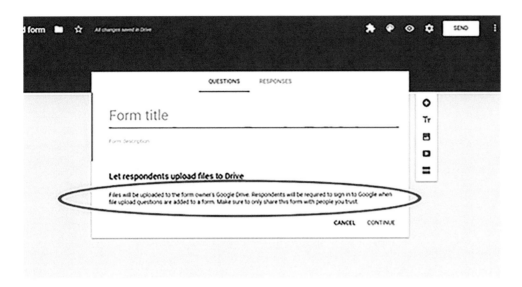

There are several options that need to be completed when using a *file upload* question. These options are highlighted in the illustration and explained below.

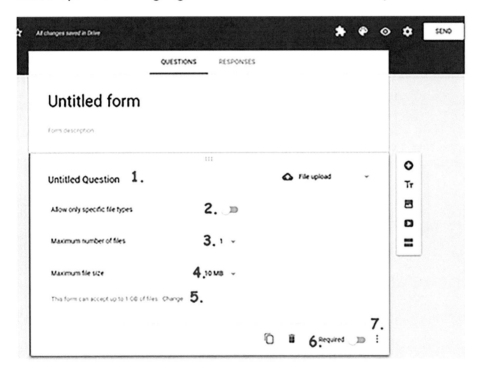

1. This is where the instructions are added, such as "Click on the ADD FILE link below and attach the homework for October 21."

2. This option enables the Form creator to allow only certain file types to be submitted by the respondent. These file types include: *document, spreadsheet, PDF file, video file, presentation, drawing, image* or *audio file.* More than one option may be selected for a Form.

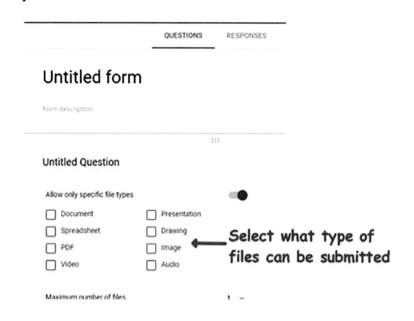

Select what type of files can be submitted

Select the number of files each Respondent can submit

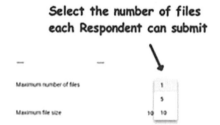

3. This option enables the Form creator to set a maximum files allowed to be submitted. The choices are: *1, 5,* or *10* individual files.

Select the maximum file size

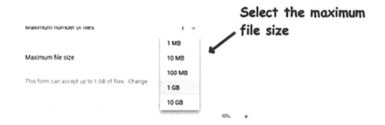

4. This option selects the maximum file size for a submission. The choices are: *1 MB, 10 MB, 100 MB, 1 GB,* or *10 GB.*

5. By default, a Form can accept up to 1 GB maximum for ALL files submitted. This setting can be changed by clicking on the hyperlinked *change* shown in the illustration to open the *Settings* dialog box for the Form.

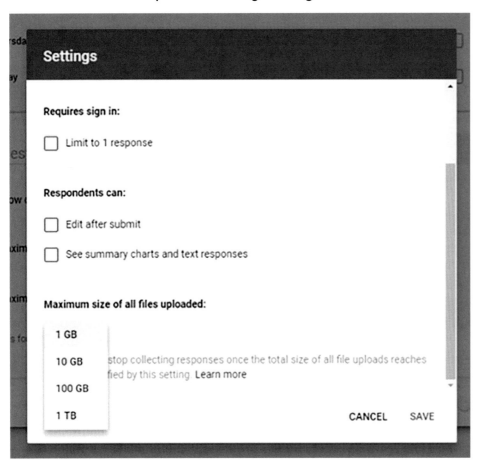

The total size can be set at *1 GB, 10 GB, 100 GB,* or *1 TB.* Keep in mind that if the creator of the Form is using a *free* Google Drive account and not paying for additional online storage, the maximum free file storage is 15 GB. Certain types of files, however, will not count toward the free file storage totals, such as:

- Google Docs, Sheets, Slides, Forms, Sites, and files in "Shared with me."

Other options available in *Settings* requires limiting the respondent to one response; allowing respondents to edit a file after it is submitted, and allowing respondents to see summary charts and text responses after the file is submitted.

6. The toggle setting for *required* means that a respondent MUST attach a file in order to submit the Form.
7. Clicking on the dots next to the *required* toggle enables adding a text description to the question, in case additional instructions are needed.

Once you have modified the settings for the *file upload* question type, the Form question is ready for use. Below is an illustration of how the respondent sees the question on the live Form.

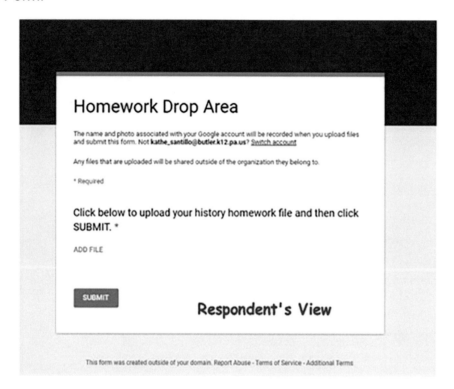

To submit a file, the respondent clicks on *ADD FILE.*

The *INSERT FILE* dialog box opens for file selection. Respondents have the option of dragging and dropping a file to submit, selecting a file from his/her Google Drive folder, or selecting a file from his/her computer, as shown below.

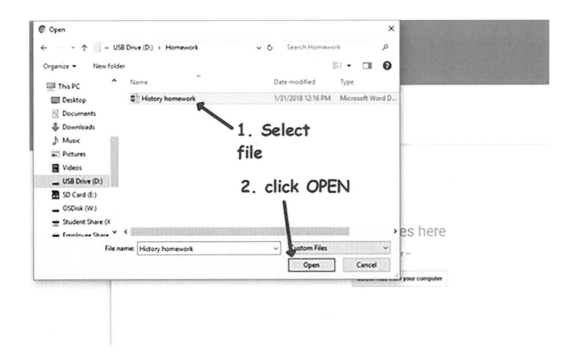

The respondent can then make sure that the correct file was selected, and select additional files, if required.

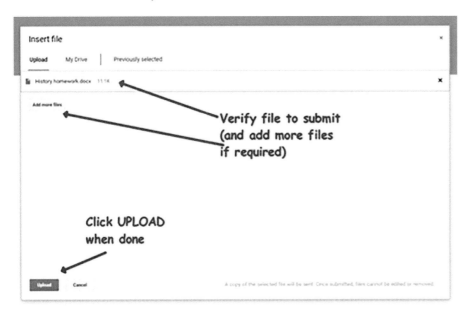

Once the files are selected, the Form returns the respondent to the original page to verify and submit the files. A confirmation response follows the submission. The response message can be customized by the Form creator

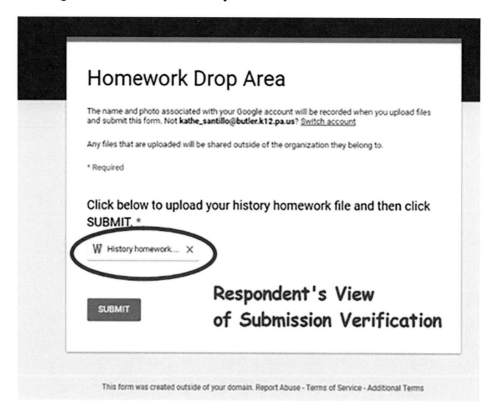

Confirmation Box

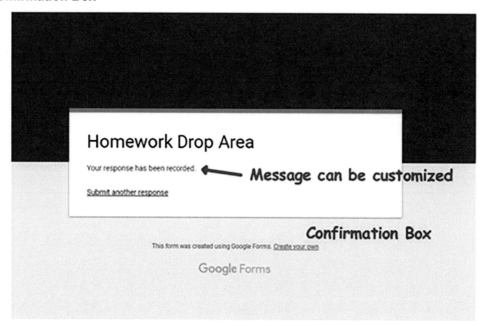

The response phrase can be customized by selecting *settings* in the upper right toolbar, clicking on *Presentation* and adding a customized confirmation response.

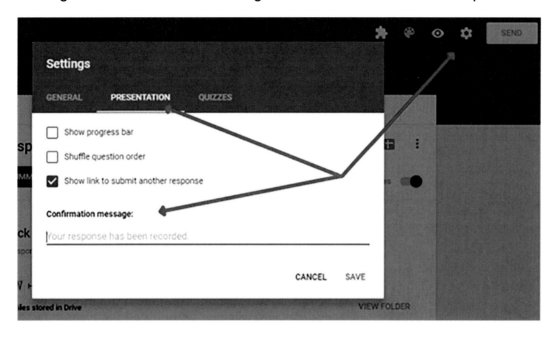

Teacher's View

Teachers can see and access respondent file submissions by opening the Form in editing view and selecting the *Responses* tab.

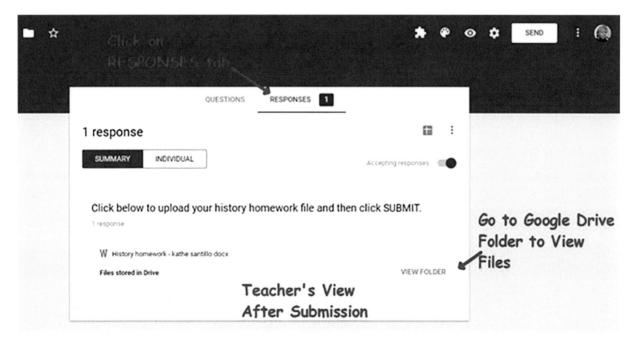

Each file submission will be listed and can be accessed by clicking on the *VIEW FOLDER* link.

NOTE – If the file submission has a deadline, such as a homework assignment, the *Accepting Responses* toggle can be turned off on the day of the deadline so no late file submissions are accepted.

Linear Scale Question Type

Select the *linear scale* (previously called *scale*) question type from the drop-down menu in the question editing area when adding a new item. Enter your criterion or question in the *question title* area, as shown in the example below. The *scale* question has a ranking of 1 to 5, however it can be modified to rank anywhere between those one and ten. For example, a question or criterion can be ranked from 1 to 5; 1 to 7; etc. Use the drop-down menu options to change this ranking scale for the question or criterion. Next, enter descriptive labels for the first (lowest) number on the scale and the last (highest) number on the scale (see example).

Linear Scale – Editing View

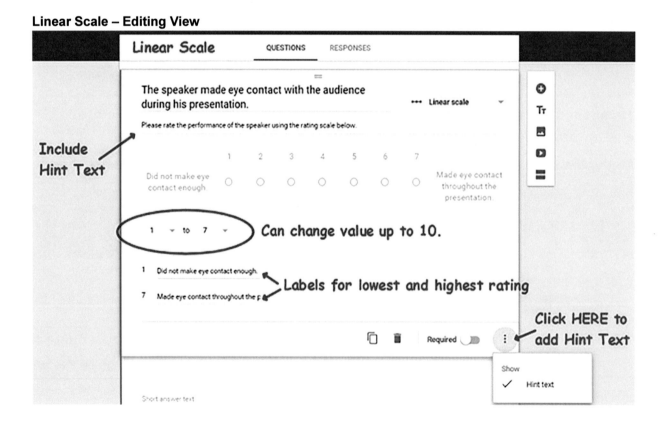

The speaker made eye contact with the audience during his presentation.

Please rate the performance of the speaker using the rating scale below.

	1	2	3	4	5	6	7	
Did not make eye contact enough.	O	O	O	O	O	O	O	Made eye contact throughout the presentation.

Multiple Choice Grid Question Type

Select the *multiple choice grid* question type (previously called grid) from the drop-down menu in the question editing area. Just like a rubric, the *multiple choice grid* question type is set up with columns and rows. A *multiple choice grid* can work as a scale for more than one question and response, as well. If used as a scale, it takes up less space on a Form than placing a scale for each question. You can also create a grid for multiple choice responses. To add additional answer choice options in either the column or row areas, click below the previous option and another answer option field will appear or hit the *Enter* key on the keyboard to advance to the next answer option. Remember, a grid works like a scale, but enables the respondent to address multiple criteria in one question, like a rubric. If a *multiple choice grid* is used as a rubric, the rows should contain the ranking criteria, and the columns should represent the ranking scale (see example below).

As with other question types, using the *Hint Text* feature is a good idea with the *multiple choice grid*. Other possible options for this question type include limiting to one response per column and shuffling the row order.

Multiple Choice Grid as a Rubric - Editing View

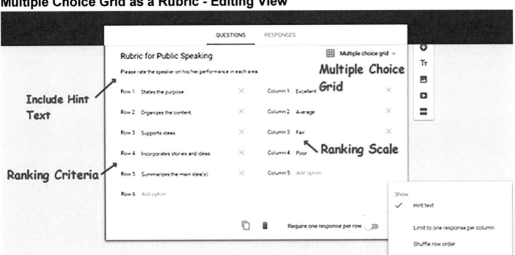

Multiple Choice Grid as a Rubric – Live View

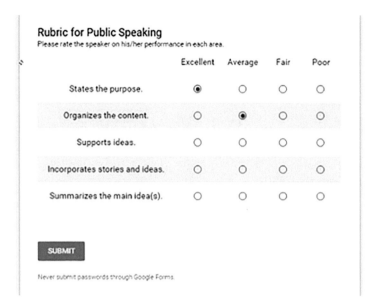

When a *multiple choice grid* is used to display multiple questions, such as a matching question, the answers can be typed in the columns of the question editing area next to the corresponding question, yet shuffled when displayed to the student by picking the *shuffle row order* option. This makes it easier to create the list, but presents the answers randomly in the selection grid of the live Form. See the examples below.

Multiple Choice Grid as a Multiple Choice Question – Editing View

The Thirteen Colonies
Match the state to its capital.

	r Annapolis	Richmond	Raleigh	Columbia	Atlant
Connecticut	○	○	○	○	○
Virginia	○	○	○	○	○
Massachusetts	○	○	○	○	○
Georgia	○	○	○	○	○
New Jersey	○	○	○	○	○
Pennsylvania	○	○	○	○	○
South Carolina	○	○	○	○	○
North Carolina	○	○	○	○	○
Rhode Island	○	○	○	○	○
New York	○	○	○	○	○
Maryland	○	○	○	○	○
New Hampshire	○	○	○	○	○
Delaware	○	○	○	○	○

Scroll bar to view all column choices

Checkbox Grid Question Type

The *checkbox grid* question type should be used when a question might have or require more than one response. An example of this might be a parent-teacher conference Form where respondents are to provide more than one response, such as time of day they may be available for the conferencing.

The checkbox grid question is displayed in rows and columns. The choices are displayed in the rows, and the options for each choice are displayed in the columns. If a Form is used to allow parents to select a day of the week, and the time or times they are available for each day, a checkbox grid should be used. See the example below:

The checkbox grid question editing area presents the fields in *Rows* and *Columns.* The question can be previewed by selecting the *Preview* icon from the top-right toolbar.

Other options can be set for checkbox grid questions, including limiting the response to one response per column, and shuffling the row placement so that questions appear differently on student screens.

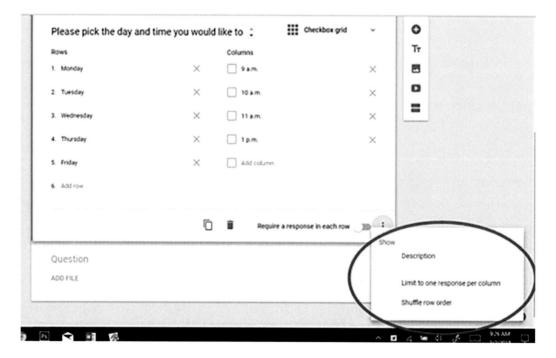

Select the *date* question type from the drop-down menu in the question editing area. There is an option to select date only or to include a time. Adding the time option with the date enables respondents to enter a start time, if needed.

Date Only – Editing View

Date Only – Live View

Date, with Time Added – Live View

Time Question Type

Select the *time* question type from the drop-down menu in the question editing area. There is an option to set the time as *duration.* If duration is not checked, the display options on the Form will show the hour, minutes, and AM or PM. If duration is checked, the display options will show hour, minutes, and seconds.

Time (Hour) – Editing View

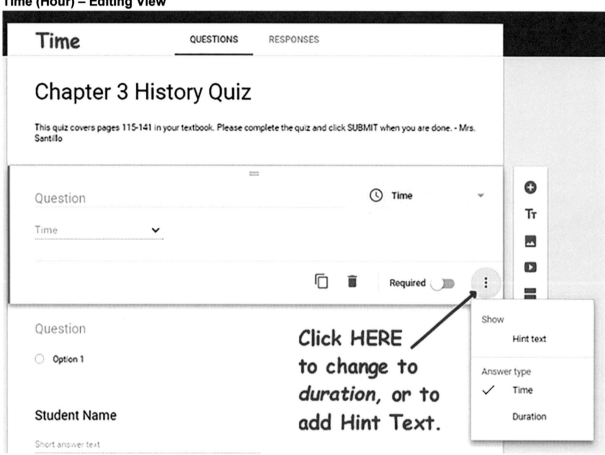

Time (Hour) – Live View

Time (Duration) – Editing View

Time (Duration) – Completed View

Back to Editing a Question

Once you have entered information into the selected question types, you can go back and edit any question, delete it, or duplicate by clicking again in the question area. You can also reorder the questions by placing the cursor over the top center of the question

area until the cursor becomes a crosshair ✛ over the two horizontal lines - ═ . Click and hold on this area to drag the question to the new position. As you drag it, the question area will be outlined in a shaded border which will be visible to help you navigate the placement. The question editing area itself will also become slightly transparent so that the placements of other question editing boxes are visible beneath it, as illustrated below.

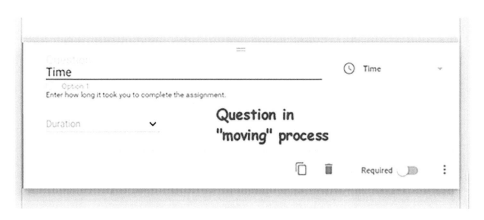

There are also tools to help manage the layout of the Form. For example, if a quiz has a lot of questions, it can be broken up into several pages. This can be helpful for students who may have issues with test anxiety. Section headers can also be added to the Form to break it into clearly defined sections. Progress bars can be added to each section so that students are aware of how much of the Form is completed as they move through a Form.

Adding a Section

A *section* can be added from the *Editing Template Toolbox* menu. Click on the *Add Section* button to begin.

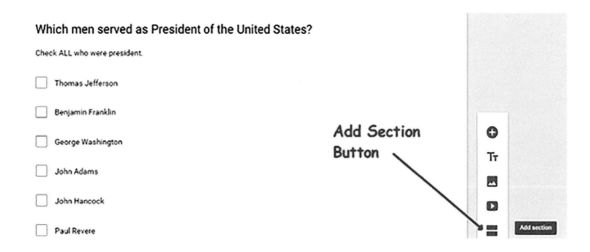

The *Add Section editing area* will open. The *Untitled Section* label is the text which will appear at the top of the next new Form page created by the *add section* option. When a section is created, it creates a new and separate page in the Form. You do not need to give a section a name (header), but if you choose not to, you must erase the text, "untitled section" from the section editing area. If you do not title a section, the Form title only will appear at the top of that section page. Titles, or *headers,* can be as simple as a page number, or they can be thematic or subject-related labels to help clarify the information on that specific section page.

Section Editing Area

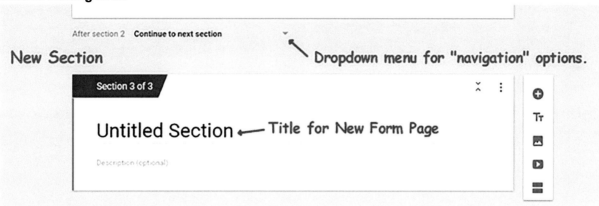

Dropdown Menu for Navigation

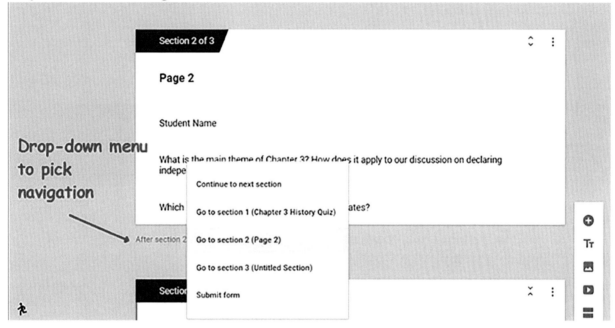

A drop-down menu will appear in the section above the new section which enables controlling where the respondent will be navigated to next, AFTER clicking on the *Next button.*

The *next* button will appear at the bottom of the first page, with the second page beginning with the question(s) after the page break. A page break can be deleted later from a Form without affecting any of the questions added. The examples on the next few pages illustrate how a Form appears when a page break with a page title is added, as well as a page break without a page title.

Live Form with Page Break and Page Title Added

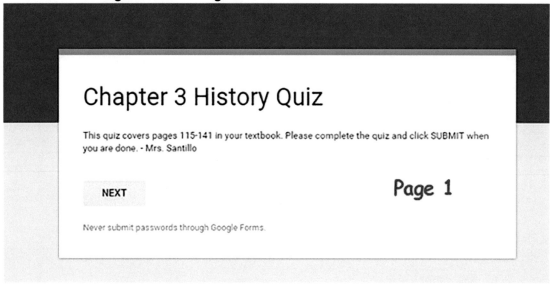

Live Form – Page after the Page Break (with Page Title)

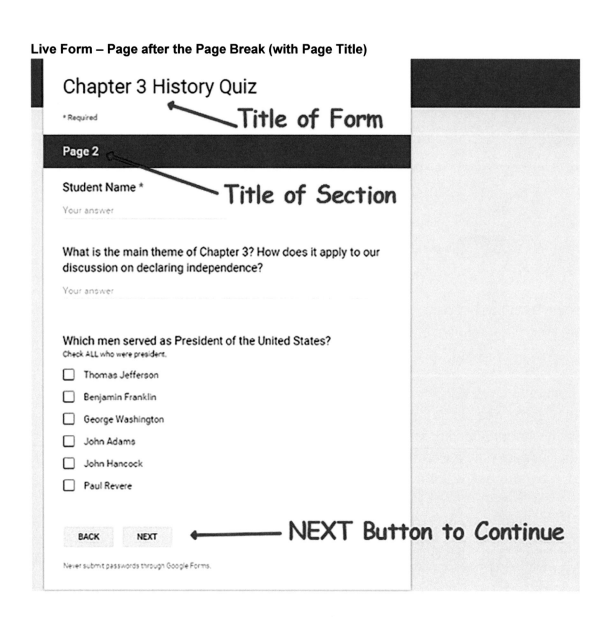

When page breaks are included in a Form, it's a good idea to use the ***progress bar*** feature. This feature lets respondents see a visual display of how much of the Form they've completed, and how much is left to complete. A progress bar can be added by clicking on the *Forms setting icon* located in the upper right corner of the Form, and then by clicking in the box next to *Show Progress Bar.*

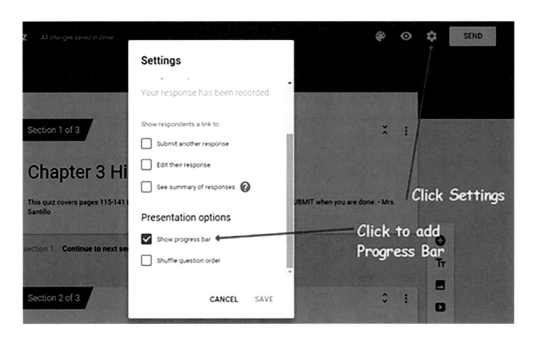

Progress Bar in Live Form

A section can be duplicated, deleted, or merged with the previous section by accessing the *Section Options Menu* in the section editing area. It can also be moved to a different location in the Form by clicking on the arrows next to the section options menu, as illustrated below.

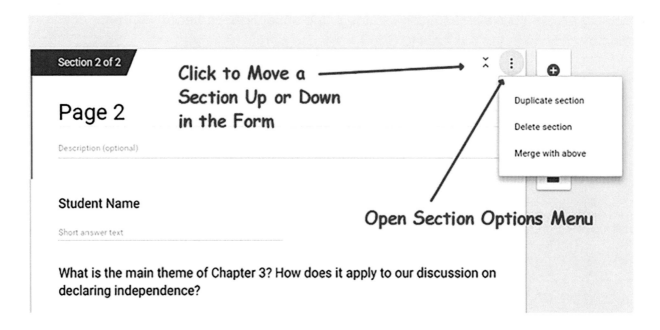

Adding Video and Images to a Google Form

Adding videos and images to a Google Form is a great way to prompt creative writing or critical thinking in student responses. A video or image coupled with a paragraph text question type is a perfect writing prompt! A VERY important note, however - Google Forms use YouTube videos. If your school district IT staff has blocked YouTube videos in your district, students will not be able to view the Form videos while on your school network.

Adding a Video

To add a video to a Form, click the *add video* button in the Editing Toolbar.
A dialog box will open. You can either search for a YouTube video from this box, or paste in a URL for a YouTube video you already located.

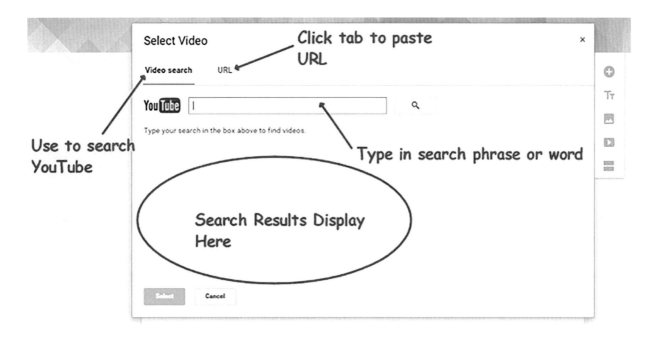

If a search is completed within the *add video* dialog box, the video cannot be previewed before it is added to the Form.

Type in a search phrase or keyword to begin searching. Choose the video from the search results list and click the SELECT button.

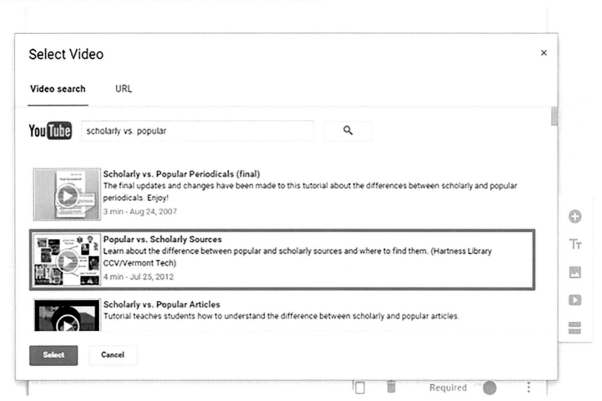

The video thumbnail now appears within the Form in an editing area similar to the question editing area. The editing options include: adding a video title; adding a video caption (appears below the video); moving the video; aligning the video in the Form;

duplicating or deleting the video; and changing the video. To see how the video will appear in the live Form, select *Preview* from the upper-right Form tools.

Add Video Editing Area

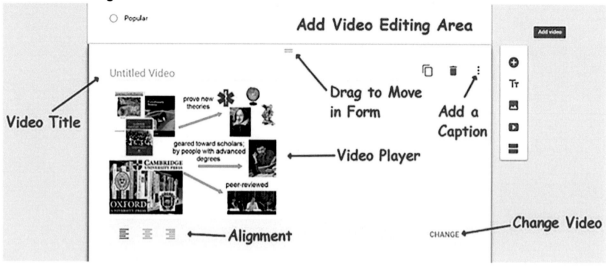

Video in Live Form

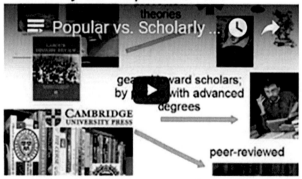

The added video plays directly within the live Form. Respondents have the same viewing options (full screen, closed caption) as they do when viewing a video from YouTube.

An image can be added by selecting the *add image* option from the Editing Toolbar.

The *add image dialog box* will open. There are several ways to add an image to a Form. **1.)** Upload the image from a file located on the computer hard drive or portable drive; **2.)** Use the computer's camera to capture an image; or **3.)** Link to an image by its URL. You can also **(4.)** locate images saved to your Google Drive account or **(5.)** *Your Albums.* There is also a *Search* link **(6.)** that enables a Google Image search directly from the *Insert Image* dialog box, or a photo can be dragged and dropped **(7.)** to the middle of the add image editing area.

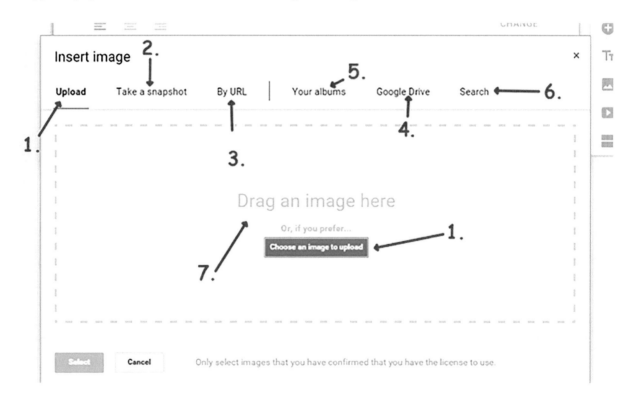

To add an image from a computer, click on the *Upload* tab, and then drag and drop the image to the center area of the dialog box or click the *choose an image to upload* button in the middle of the screen. If this method is used, you will be prompted to pick an image file from a file dialog box. Select the image file and click *open* to proceed, as shown below.

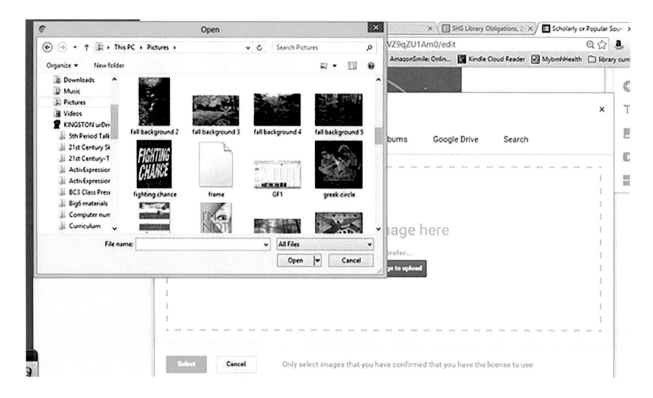

Next, the add image editing area will open. The *image title* **(1.)** appears above the image **(2.)** itself. The *hover text* **(6.)** will appear when the mouse cursor moves over the image. The image can also be aligned left, right or center **(3.)** on the Form page. The image can be duplicated **(4.),** deleted **(5.),** or changed **(7.).** The section can also be moved **(8.)**, as with any question section.

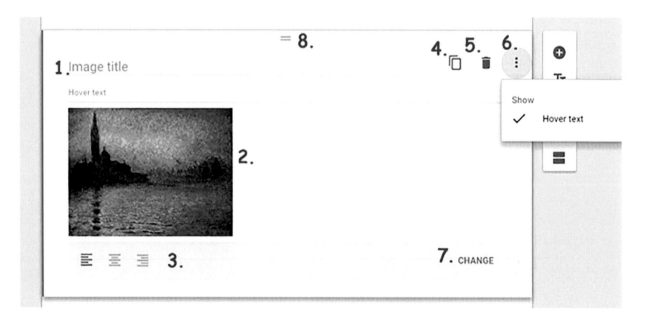

Live Form with Image and Paragraph Question Type

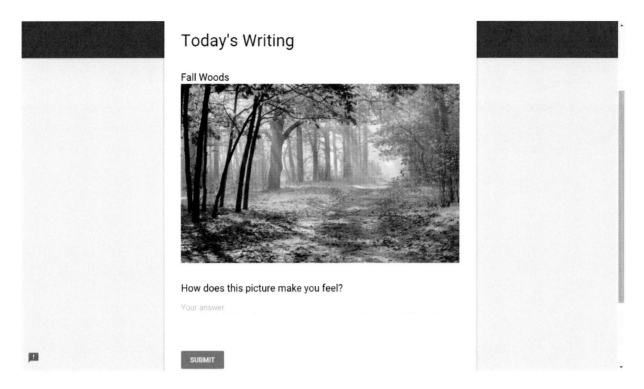

Changing the Way a Form Looks

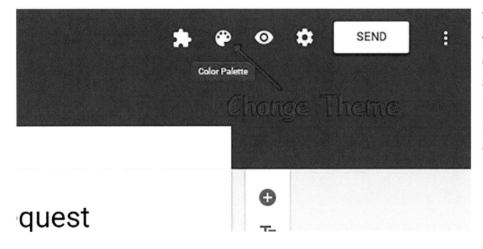

The appearance, or theme of a Form can be changed at any time using the *Color Palette* option in the top right tool area.

When opened, the menu displays color circles, which let you quickly change the background color of the Form theme. There is also an option to use an illustrated background. To select this option, click on the bottom right corner icon to access the template choices, or to use your own photo.

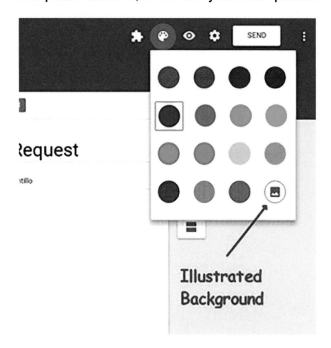

The selection of themes is nice. My only complaint is that there are not many that are education or school-based, but the collection of seasonal and patterned themes makes up for it a bit. You can browse the theme templates from the theme dialog box, or you can upload your own photo to use as a background.

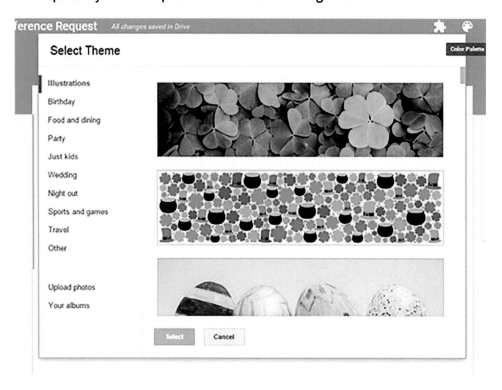

Select *Upload Photos* from the *Select Theme* box. The photo you use must be at least 800 x 200 pixels in size.

The photo file can be dragged and dropped in the center area, or simply click on the button labeled, *Select a Photo from Your Computer*.

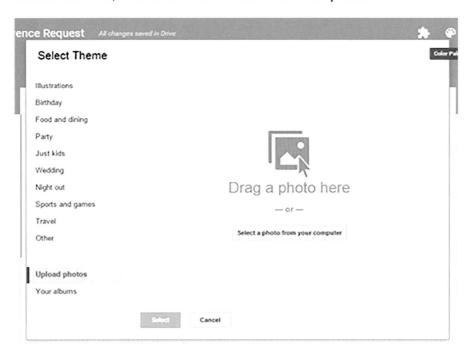

Select the photo from your folder. The photo will open in the dialog box with a cropping box centered in it. This cropping box will be the portion of the photo which is displayed on the Form. Center the cropping area where you want it and click *Select*.

The theme is now applied to your Form.

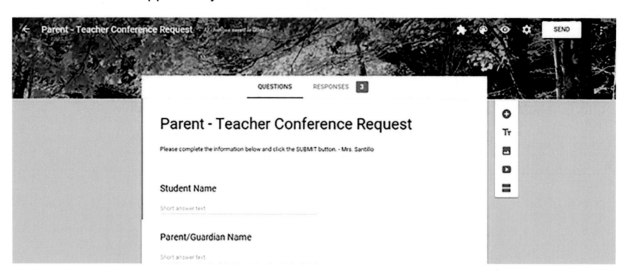

Chapter 4: The Form Settings

The Google Form settings let you manage and control the Form and Form responses. There are two areas where Form settings can be changed, as illustrated in the image below. Both settings menus are located in the top right corner of the Form editing template.

Let's look at each of the toolbar menu setting options and their uses.

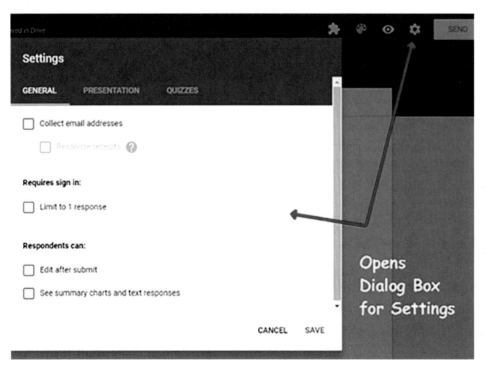

Clicking on *Settings* opens a dialog box where submission and presentation changes can be made.

Those options are divided into three categories. These were discussed earlier in this book, but bear repeating here: The three categories again are: **General, Presentation,** and **Quizzes**. Each area has its own settings. The *General* settings are default settings for ALL Forms created.

The options under the *General* settings tab are:

Collect email addresses – This option collects the email addresses of respondents who submit a completed Form.

Response Receipts – If *collect email addresses* is activated, when this feature is enabled all respondents will receive a copy of their responses.

Limit to One Response – If this setting is selected, respondents must be signed in to a Google account. You could use this if your students have individual Google accounts created, or your school district uses Google for Education. If parents are asked to create Google accounts at the beginning of the year, using this feature on a Form can also limit each parent to one submission.

Respondents Can Edit After Submit – This enables respondents to change their answers after they've submitted them. If the *Edit Their Response* has been enabled, a respondent can click on the "edit your response" link on the Form Confirmation Page to make changes to the submission. The Form will reopen, with the respondent's earlier answers/information. The respondent can then make changes and re-submit the new response. The new response does NOT replace the earlier submission in the destination spreadsheet, but the timestamp will distinguish the edited response from the original one.

Respondents Can See Summary Charts and Text Responses – Enables respondents to see a summary of everyone's responses. This is a great option to enable if you would like to share immediate results with students in a graphic illustration. It's perfect for showing students or respondents immediate results from a poll or survey. Keep in mind that textual responses (*short answer* and *paragraph*) are displayed as such – just text; however *multiple choice, checkboxes,* and other question types are displayed in a pie chart format, as shown in the illustration below:

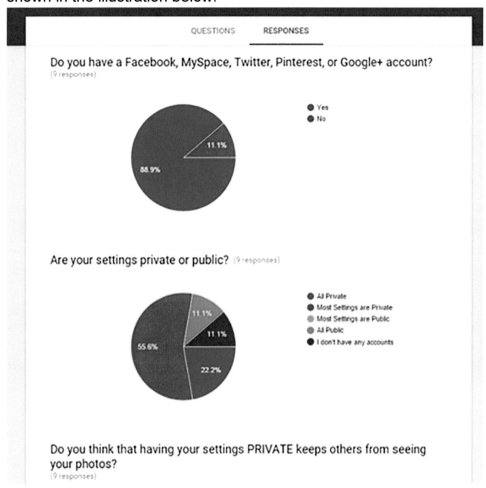

***Presentation Settings*:**

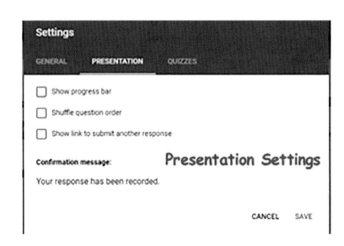

Confirmation Page Message – Create a unique message here that the respondents will see after they complete the Form and click the SUBMIT button to send the completed Form. This message can provide the respondent with additional information he/she may need, such as when a grade will be returned for the work; additional contact information for you; or a simple thank you for completing a survey or poll.

64

Show Link to Submit Another Response – Displays the link to the Form on the confirmation page which allows respondents to submit another response.

Show Progress Bar - This presentation option include adds a *progress bar* to the Form to be displayed on longer Forms which have been divided into sections using the *add section* option. The progress bar displays the percentage of the Form that was completed on each section page. A progress bar can let respondents see how much of a Form they've completed.
Shuffle Question Order is a good option to use if students will be sitting in close proximity of each other during the completion of a test or quiz created on a Form.

When settings are enabled which allow respondents to submit another response; edit a response; or view a summary of responses after submitting the Form, links will appear on the Confirmation Page, as is shown in the illustration below. The Confirmation Page appears after the respondent clicks the SUBMIT button at the bottom of a Form.

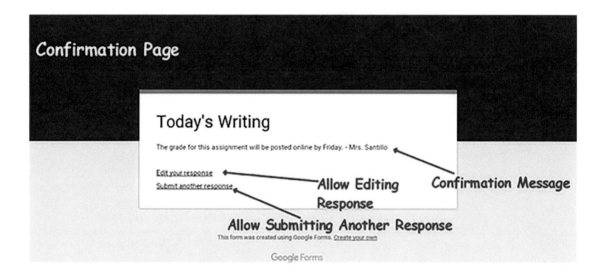

Quizzes Settings:

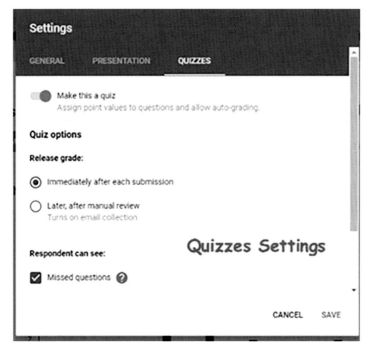

Make This a Quiz – Selecting this toggle option enables assigning a point value to each question and enables auto-grading. The point value is actually assigned to each question during the creation of the quiz Form.

Release Grade – If a Form is designated a quiz, the Form creator can select between *immediately after each submission* or *later, after manual review.* Selecting the "later" option turns on the email collection feature of the Form.

Respondent Can See Missed Questions – Selecting this enables respondents to immediately see the results of the quiz. Each missed question is highlighted, and the correct answer is displayed.

More Settings

Additional settings for a Form are located under the *More Settings* icon. These were explained earlier, but a couple of these options are worth repeating and elaborating on.

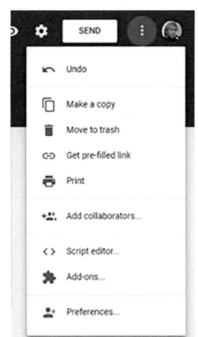

For example, the **_Print_** option creates a hands-on, printed version of a Form. The printed version can be used as a back-up plan, in case of a technology failure. Obviously, the responses will not be automatically fed into the destination spreadsheet when a printed version is used, but, in a pinch, or if a respondent is technophobic, you have the printed Form as an option. Printed copies of your Forms can be kept on file _just in case_ your Google Drive files become corrupted or there is a serious failure on Google's part. That way, if the Form has to be re-created, the printout can be your guide.

The **_add-ons_** option lets you search for and add additional software programs that work together with Google Forms to extend a Form's functionality. Add-ons will be discussed later.

The **_preferences_** option enables default settings to be applied to every Form created, such as collecting the email addresses of respondents or setting the default point value of questions added to a Form.

Add Collaborators to a Form

Selecting *Add Collaborators* opens the *Sharing Settings*. The Sharing Settings let you control who can edit and/or view the Form; share the Form via social media; change privacy settings; and invite others to collaborate on the Form. The share settings permit others to edit the Form. Collaborators will also be able to view the Form responses, as well.

The Form can be shared with anyone on the Web; with anyone who has the Form link; or with individuals you selectively allow.

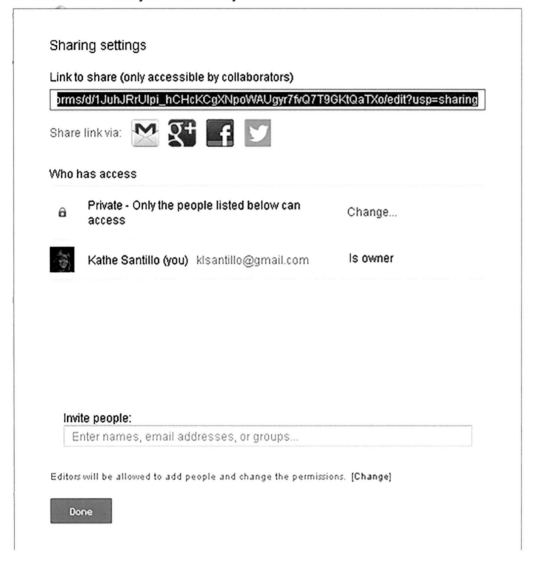

Send Form

The *Send Form* option displays the Form link; provides the Form html embed code; enables social media sharing; provides an area for sending the Form via email; and provides a link to invite Form collaborators.

Make a Copy of a Form

This creates a duplicate copy of the Google Form and the destination response spreadsheet. This is a very handy feature to use to quickly create multiple identical Forms for use in several classes so that responses can be stored in separate spreadsheets, or if minor modifications need to be made to a spreadsheet but you don't want to change the original Form.

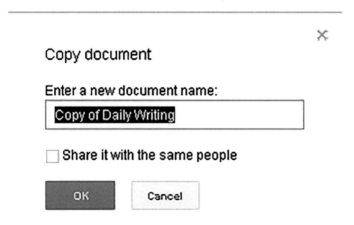

Move to Folder

This option lets you move both the Google Form and the destination response spreadsheet to a different folder within your Google Drive.

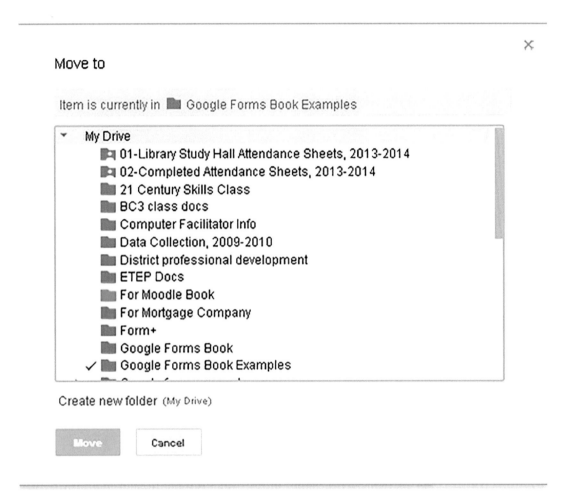

Sharing the Form with SEND

The *Send* button opens a *Send Form* dialog box so the Form can be shared with others for completion. This is different from sharing with collaborators.

Sharing with collaborators enables another person to view responses and edit the Form. Sharing the Form via the *Send* button enables *viewing and completing* the Form.

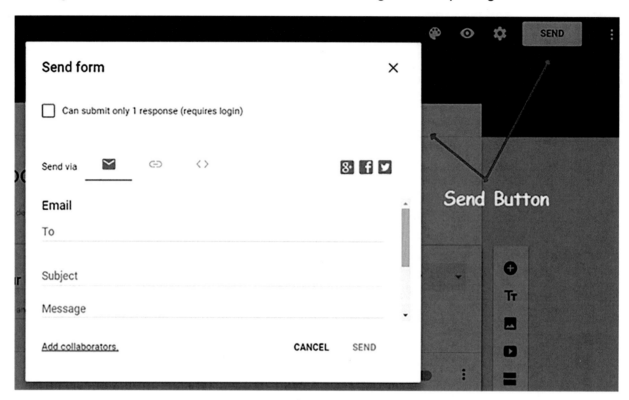

There are several options for sharing a Form. To select the method for sharing you wish to use, click on the icon in the "send via" area, as illustrated below.

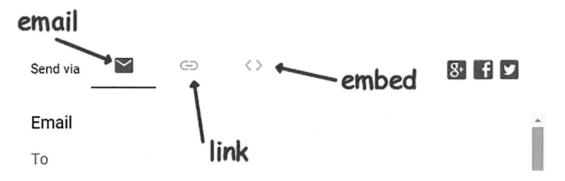

When an icon is selected, the options for that method of sharing will be displayed in the dialog box.

The *Share via email* option lets you send the Form to the people you want to complete it through email. This method includes the option of placing the live Form directly in the body of the email, so no link is needed.

This method works very well for parent and staff communications because the Form can be completed quickly and easily. The email includes an alternative link to the Form, just in case the respondent has trouble viewing it in the email environment.

Share via Email

Share via Link

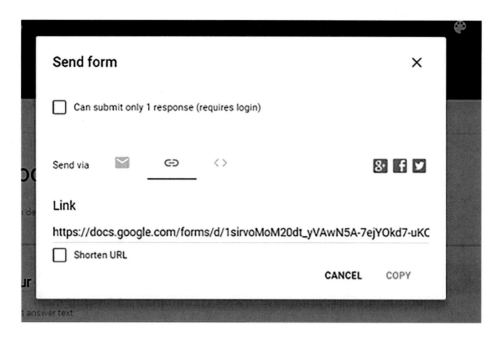

The *share via link* option provides the Form creator with a unique link to the live Form. This link can be shared on Websites, through emails, etc. The generated link is fairly lengthy, so Google provides a checkbox to shorten the link to a more manageable length. If the *shorten URL* checkbox is toggled, a shorter URL appears, which can be copied and pasted as needed.

Share via Embed

Send form   ✕

☐ Can submit only 1 response (requires login)

Send via   ✉   ⌐   ‹ ›   8⁺ f 𝕐

Embed HTML

<iframe src="https://docs.google.com/forms/d/1sirvoMoM20dt_yVAwN5A-7

Width 760 px   Height 500 px

CANCEL   COPY

The *share via embed* option lets the Form creator share a Form by embedding it in another Web page, such as a class Website or parent page. When a Form is embedded, it appears as the live Form on that Web page.

Share via Social Media

 Creators also have the option to share a Form through social media (*Google +, Facebook* and *Twitter).* If this option is selected, the Form creator is directed to log in to the specific social media tool, and then follow directions to share the Form through that medium.

Chapter 5: The Responses Tab

The *Responses Tab* contains the settings and options for viewing and receiving Form responses in the destination spreadsheet. Once the Form begins receiving responses, the responses tab also enables viewing a quick summary of the received responses.

The *Responses Tab* contains different options if the Form was created as a quiz. See Chapter 8 for a detailed description of creating a Form as a quiz and the quiz *Responses Tab.*

It is best to designate a spreadsheet for the responses when the Form is initially created. Individual responses can be viewed and assessed through the Form, however you must view each one at a time. If the responses go to a spreadsheet, all responses are visible in one area. Using the Form to store responses works well if the Form is just being used for a quick poll or survey to introduce a lesson, but if individual grades are being assessed from the Form responses, you may prefer to use a spreadsheet destination assigned to the Form. Also, many add-ons like *Flubaroo* and *Autocrat,* which will be discussed in this book, require a destination spreadsheet to run.

The Responses Tab

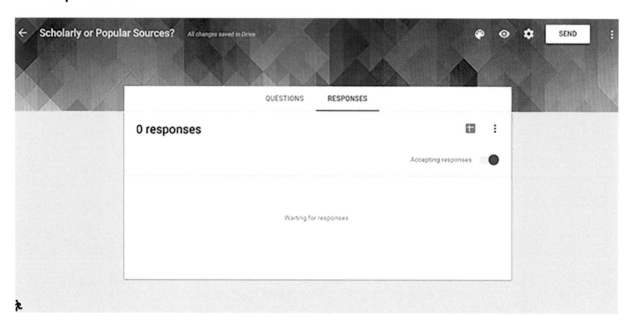

Accepting/Not Accepting Responses

This setting lets the Form creator "turn on" or "turn off" whether a student can submit a completed Form and responses. This is a great way to control late submissions of homework or quizzes because it prevents submission after a designated date.

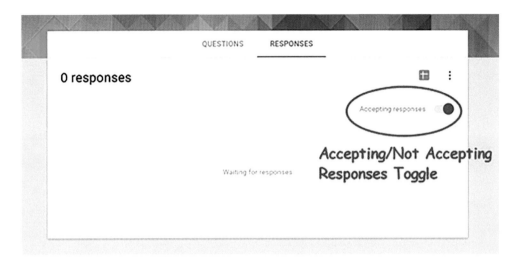

If the toggle is set to *not accepting responses,* a message will be displayed to the respondent. The default message can be edited with a personal message, as illustrated below in the second graphic.

Default Message

Customized Message

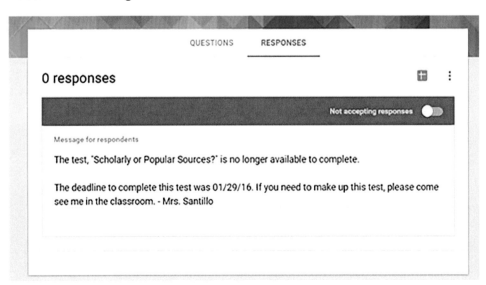

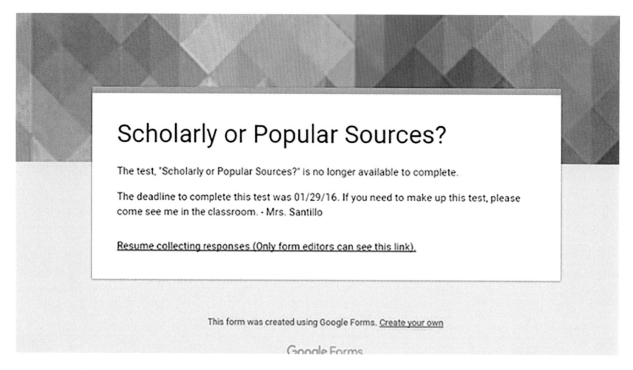

Summary of Responses and Individual Responses

There are two available options for viewing the responses from most Forms, but there are three if the Form uses the *Quizzes* settings. Google Forms provides an option to view individual responses (2.) to a Form as well as the summary of responses (1.). The active option is highlighted in blue to show which option is open.

Viewing Summary of Responses

The *summary of responses,* as mentioned earlier in this book, presents a graphic overview of the Form responses. In the summary of responses area, responses will be presented in pie chart or bar graph format. Keep in mind, if the Form is being used as an assessment tool, such as a quiz or test, the summary of responses does not show whether an answer is correct or incorrect. It simply shows the percentage of respondents who selected an answer.

The summary of responses will be visible when the Responses tab is selected, as long as the Form has been completed by some respondents. That means that the summary of responses area will remain empty until responses are received. If a Form has received responses from questions that require the respondent to enter text, such as the *short answer* or *paragraph* question type, the responses will not be displayed in a graphic, but will simply be listed as a text entry, as illustrated with the student names in the images below.

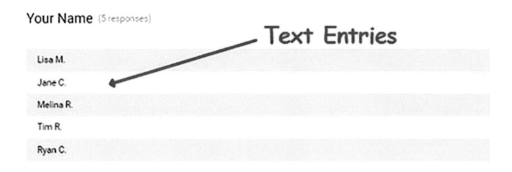

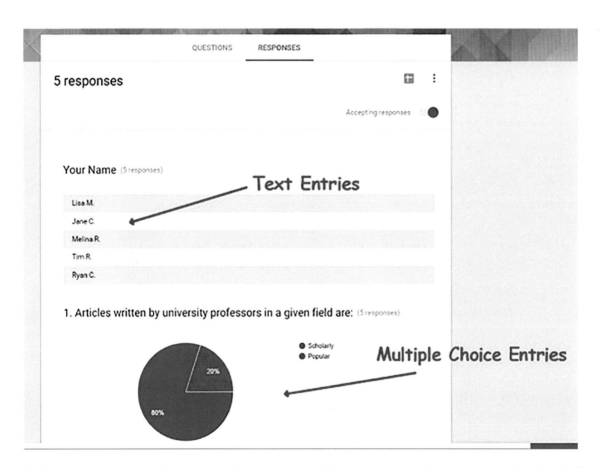

A destination spreadsheet can be created *after* responses have been submitted, if desired, by clicking on the little green spreadsheet icon and selecting where the responses should go – a new spreadsheet or an existing one.

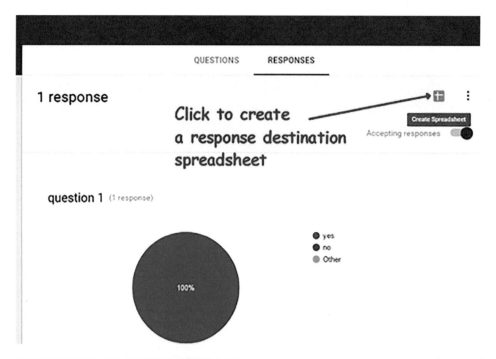

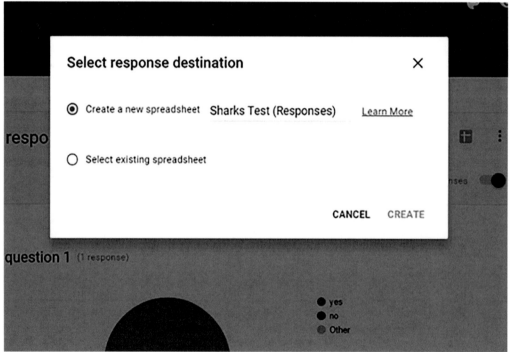

If using a Form as a poll or survey, the summary of responses is a great way to quickly show students the results. One way to show results immediately is to project the destination spreadsheet on an interactive whiteboard or screen as students submit their responses. Students will be able to see the answers populate the open spreadsheet. After all students responses are submitted, the option to view the summary of responses can be selected from the destination spreadsheet, which will open the summary of responses graphic.

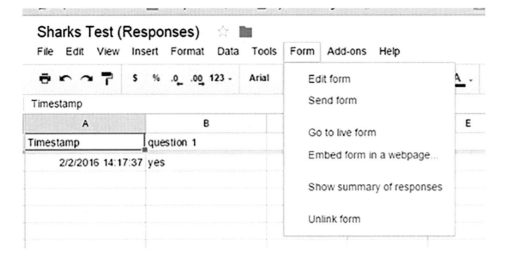

Viewing Individual Responses

Individual students responses can be viewed, printed or deleted directly from the Form. To view individual responses, select the *Responses Tab,* and then select the *individual* option. Each individual response can be printed from this area if you prefer to keep a hard copy of the assessment or distribute it to students or parents.

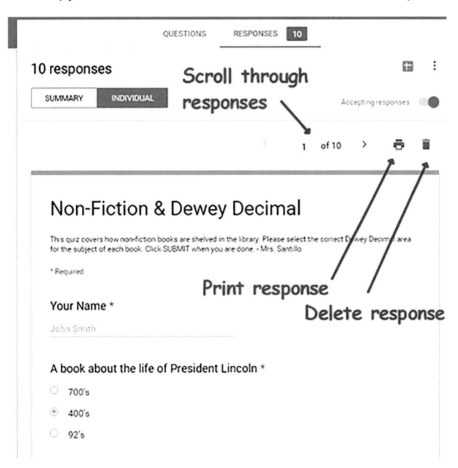

Responses Options

There are several options available under the Responses tab. To open the options, click on the vertical dots next to the green spreadsheet icon.

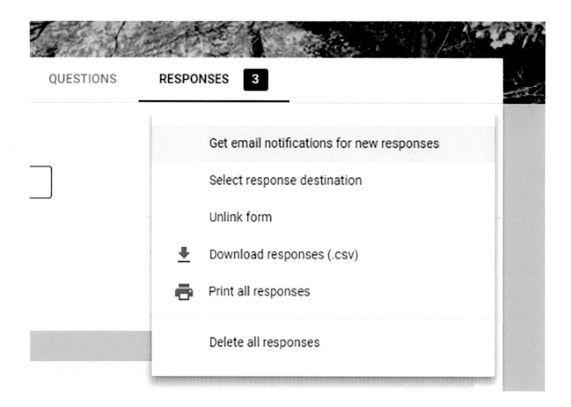

The Responses options are:

   Get Email Notifications for New Responses – This option enables an email notification be sent to the Form creator each time a Form is submitted.

Select Response Destination – If this option is selected, the *select response destination* dialog box opens, which is the same dialog box used when the initial spreadsheet destination is created. The destination spreadsheet can be changed at any time. Note – if you change the destination spreadsheet, the old as well as the new responses will move there, but any responses received *after* a new destination was created will NOT be on the old destination spreadsheet. So, if five students submit responses, and then the destination spreadsheet is changed, the responses from student 6+ will not show up in the first spreadsheet, but ALL the responses for students 1-6+ will show up in the new destination spreadsheet.

Unlink Form - . This option enables unlinking a destination spreadsheet from a Form. Why is this useful? Well, if a test, poll, etc., is created that is needed for multiple classes, the Form can be unlinked from one destination spreadsheet and a new destination spreadsheet can be created and named for each class, keeping the responses separate. This way, a new Form does not have to be created for each class. This could also be done if a Form is used each year, but you do not want to delete the previous years' responses.

Download Responses – This option enables downloading the Form responses as a .csv file, which can be opened in *Microsoft Excel*, as well as other software programs.

Print All Responses – This option prints each individual Form response as opposed to the collection of Form responses if responses were printed from the Destination Spreadsheet.

Delete All Responses – This option deletes all existing responses in the destination spreadsheet. Like the *unlink form* option, this lets a Form be used again, however any past responses are NOT saved for review. So, if you want to keep old responses in another spreadsheet, the *unlink* option and the *create a new spreadsheet* option should be used instead of this option.

Deleting a Form or Form Responses

If a destination spreadsheet is deleted, it does not delete the Form; and if a Form is deleted, it will not delete the spreadsheet. If a Form is deleted, the destination spreadsheet will still be available for review or assessment.

When the spreadsheet is deleted, the Form will hold onto the responses, and, if the Form is used again and new responses are collected in a *new* spreadsheet, the old responses will appear with the new ones. That is why it is important to *unlink* a spreadsheet if you prefer to keep responses separate.

Responses can be deleted from a Form so that the Form can be re-used. Individual responses cannot be deleted. The option to delete Form responses means that ALL responses to the Form will disappear. As mentioned earlier, this does not affect the destination spreadsheet.

Re-Using a Form

To re-use a Form, follow these instructions:

1. Unlink the Form from its destination spreadsheet.
2. Delete the responses from the Form.
3. Create or select a new destination spreadsheet for the next round of responses.

Chapter 6: Branching a Form

What is Branching?

Branching a Form is a way of setting up the Form so that it sends respondents to a specific section based on the response given to a question. An example of this might be setting up a Form where the first question is "What is your favorite pet?" If the answer options are *dog, cat, snake, rodent,* and the student picks "dog", the Form will direct the student to dog-specific questions, whereas the student who selected "cat" would be directed to cat-specific questions.

Creating a Branched Question

First, it's important to note that the only two question types you can use to *lead* the respondent to the appropriate branched section are: *multiple choice* and *choose from a list.*

To begin a branched Form, create the lead question, as illustrated below, and then click on the vertical dots in the right corner of the question editing area to enable *Go to Section Based on Answer.*

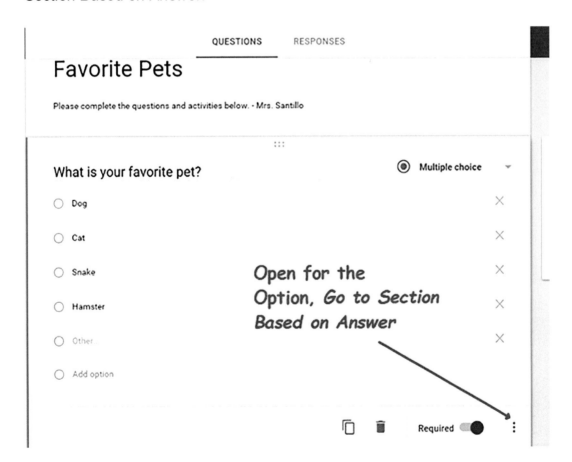

When the *Go to Section Based on Answer* option is selected, a check mark will appear next to it.

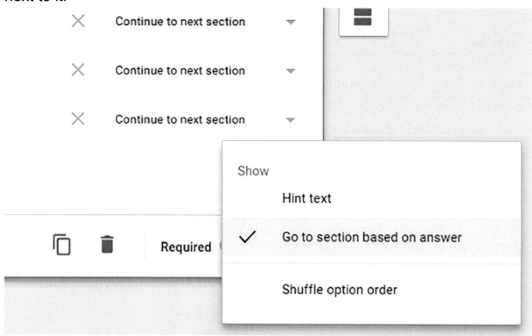

Once the option is selected, each answer option will now have a section navigation option as well, as shown below:

Now a section needs to be created for each answer option. To create a section, click on the *Add Section* icon in the *editing toolbar.* It's better to create all of the sections at once, so each is available on the drop-down list of sections in the section navigation area.

An untitled section will open.

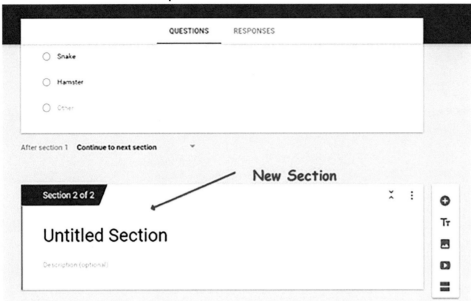

It's easier to name each section something similar to its answer option. For example, the section created for the "dog" answer choice could be titled, "Dogs". Once the new section has been created and named, you can add specific questions to it by clicking the *Add Question* icon in the *editing toolbar.*

Once each branching section is created, return to the section navigation area and select the correct navigation option for each answer. In the example below, I would select *Go to section 2 (Dogs)* next to the answer option, *Dog,* and so on for each possible answer, as shown in the second illustration.

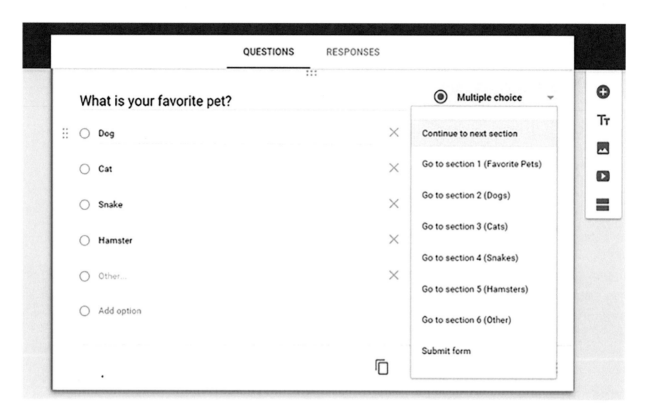

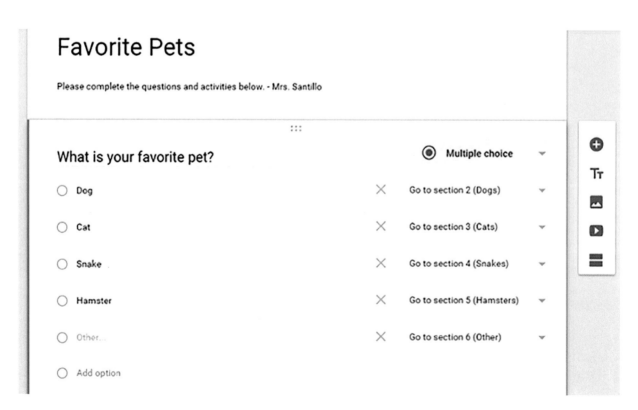

Navigating From a Form Section

So, now that the Form knows where to send the respondent after he answers the *first* question, you now must tell the Form where to send the respondent after he has finished the answers in the branched section. The Form can be set up to send all respondents to another section of general questions after completing the section-specific ones, or the Form can send the respondent to the SUBMIT section after the specific questions are answered.

To direct the respondent to the designated section *after* the branched section is completed, use the drop down menu located under the last question of the branched section, as shown below.

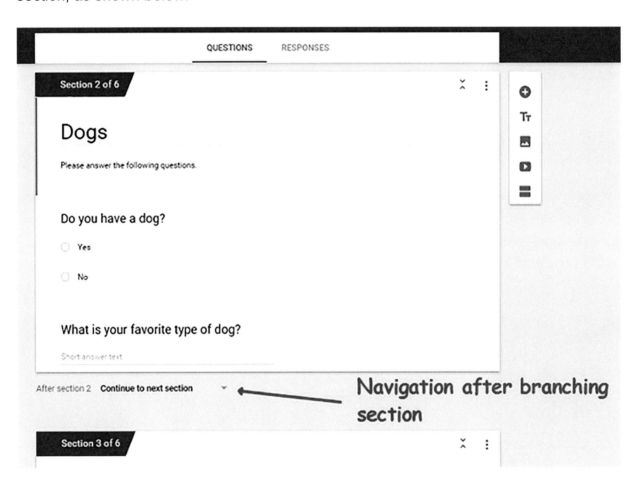

This navigation menu lets the Form creator direct the respondent to another area of the Form, or to the submission section.

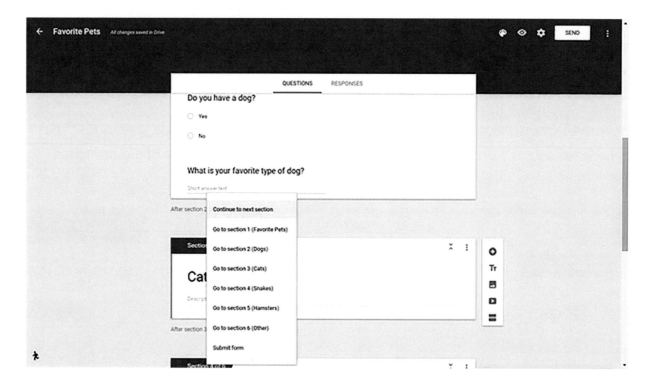

Make sure to always try a branched Form first before your students complete it to make sure the navigation paths are all correct. You can try out a Form using the *Preview* area in the upper-right tool area.

Chapter 7: Making the Destination Spreadsheet Work for You

The destination spreadsheet can be much more than just the holding point for the Form responses. There are several tricks a Form creator can use to make it quicker and easier to assess Form responses. Some of these tricks require spreadsheet *add-ons*, a few of which will be discussed in detail later.

All of these next tips and tricks are created and implemented in the destination spreadsheet itself – *not* in the Form. Remember, your Form is actually two parts – the Form itself that is completed by respondents, and the destination spreadsheet where all of the responses go when the Form is submitted. Both files are kept in with your Google Drive files, and each can be opened and edited independently of each other.

Using Conditional Formatting

Conditional formatting can be added to the spreadsheet cells as a way to quickly assess the responses received from the Form. This is done by designating that either the text in the specific cell or the background of the cell turn a certain color

Conditional formatting can be used to aid in the assessment of the responses, however a much quicker method for grading responses can be implemented using the add-on, *Flubaroo.*

By adding conditional formatting, you can quickly see if a cell (response) contains the correct or incorrect information/answer. Of course, setting up the Form using the *Quizzes* settings works for this, too, depending on your own preference.

To access the conditional formatting dialog rules box, open the destination spreadsheet and click on the *format* option in the top tool bar, and select *Conditional formatting…*

Opening Conditional Formatting

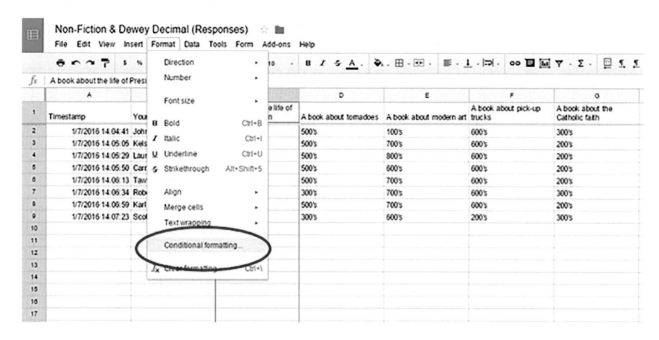

Conditional Formatting Dialog Box

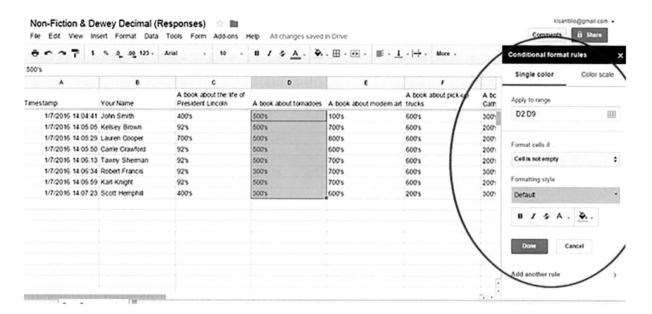

Conditional formatting can be set up before or after responses are sent to the spreadsheet. It can be added to a single cell or a column of responses, depending on your need.

So how does conditional formatting work? When conditional formatting is applied, the cell or cells where the conditional formatting is used will change color (background or text) depending on whether a specific word or number appears, or doesn't appear, based on how the conditional formatting was set up. This quickly alerts you, the teacher that something is incorrect/correct, depending on how the condition was set up.

Here are the features of the *Conditional Formatting Rules Dialog Box.*

1. This option allows for setting up the conditional formatting to color a cell in one single color or a range of color.

2. This area shows the range of cells affected by the conditional formatting.

3. The exceptions list is here. Choose from the list the condition that will cause the cell or text to change color. The options are:

      a. cell is empty
      b. cell is not empty
      c. text contains
      d. text does not contain
      e. text starts with
      f. text ends with
      g. text is exactly
      h. date is
      i. date is before
      j. date is after
      k. greater than
      l. greater than or equal to
      m. less than
      n. less than or equal
      o. is equal to
      p. is not equal to
      q. is between
      r. is not between
      s. custom formula is…

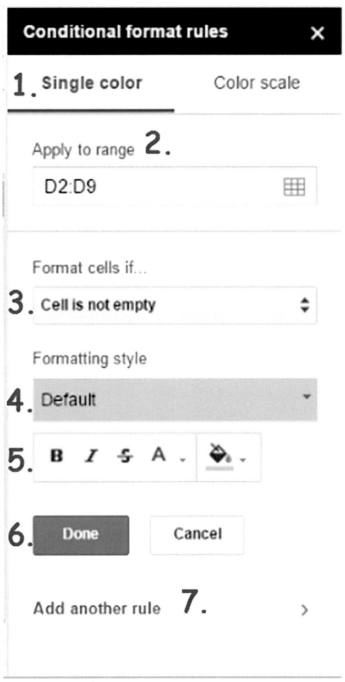

4. Select the color for the background or for the text, or create a custom color option.

5. This option changes the formatting of the text that appears in the cell or column if the designated conditions have been met.

6. Click DONE when finished with the conditional formatting.

7. *Add Another Rule* to another cell or column of cells before completing the conditional formatting set up.

If the Form being used is a long one with many answer options, I would recommend using the *Quizzes* settings in Forms or *Flubaroo* to assess and grade the assignment instead of conditional formatting. Why? Because each column of cells must be set up with the conditional formatting and it can take time. The biggest reason to use the *Quizzes* settings or *Flubaroo* over conditional formatting for grading is that they automatically generates a percentage correct score. If conditional formatting is used, the grade must be calculated manually by you.

So what's a good reason for using conditional formatting with the Form destination spreadsheet? There are many! One example might be if a Form is being used as a sign up sheet for parent conferences. A question could be added to the Form about whether the parent has "any issues of concern". Conditional formatting could be applied to that column to change the background color for any parents who add a response to that specific question (or include a specific word in the response) to make the response stand out easily on the spreadsheet. I use conditional formatting in my attendance spreadsheet when students come to the library from study hall on a reference pass, to alert me that the students should be working on a research assignment. Conditional formatting can be also used in the *timestamp* column that appears in every spreadsheet to highlight late assignment submissions. If you can think of a condition you want to be alerted to, you can create it in conditional formatting.

If you are setting up conditional formatting *after* responses have been submitted, make sure you select ALL the cells in that column which have a response, and make sure you DO NOT select the top of the column which displays the question, because the conditional formatting will be applied to the question as well.

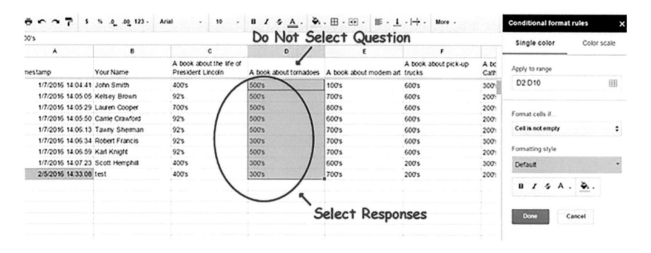

Spreadsheet Settings to Make Life Easier

Besides conditional formatting, there are other spreadsheet settings that can be used with the destination spreadsheet to make monitoring student responses easier and more efficient.

Text Wrapping

Text wrapping makes it easier to read the questions at the top of the spreadsheet columns. These are the questions that were entered automatically into the destination spreadsheet when the Form was initially created. If an entire column is text-wrapped, longer student responses are also easier to read.

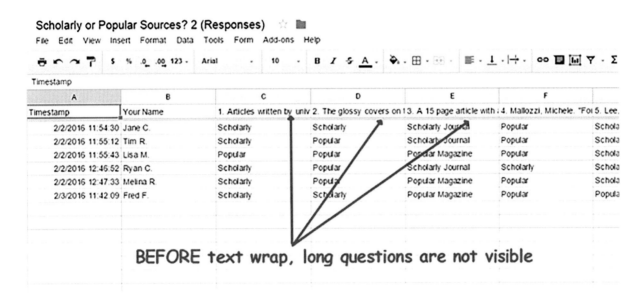

BEFORE text wrap, long questions are not visible

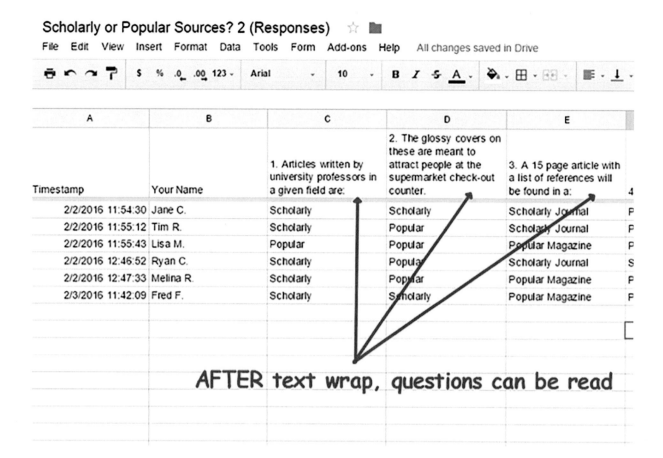

AFTER text wrap, questions can be read

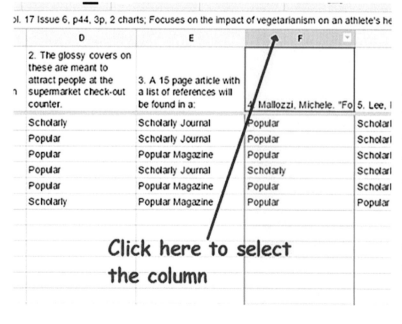

Click here to select the column

Text wrapping can be added to a column by selecting the column and adding the text wrap feature, either through the *Format* (FORMAT – TEXT WRAPPING – WRAP) in the top toolbar, or by using the text wrap icon at the top of the spreadsheet.

Click at the top of each column to select the specific column first.

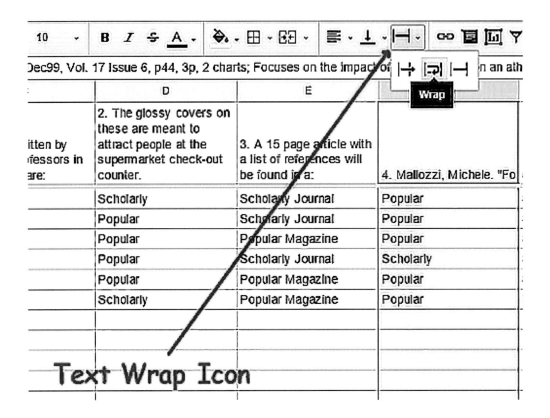

Text Wrap Icon

Notification Rules

Notification rules can be set to notify the teacher when a Form has been completed and submitted by a student. To enable notification rules, go to TOOLS – NOTIFICATION RULES… in the top toolbar of the destination spreadsheet. A dialog box will open.

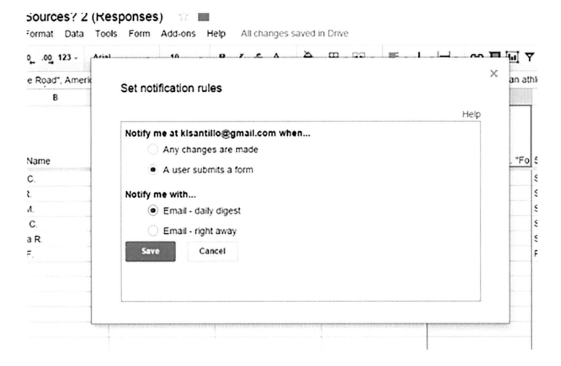

If you want to be notified when a Form is submitted, select *A User Submits a Form* in the dialog box. There are two methods for email notification – right away or a daily digest. The "right away" option notifies you each time a Form is submitted, as soon as it is submitted. The "daily digest" option emails a list of submissions each day.

Notification rules are great to use with Forms for parent-teacher conferences, meeting requests, workshop enrollment, etc., or anything that may require your attention right away.

Form Tools in the Destination Spreadsheet

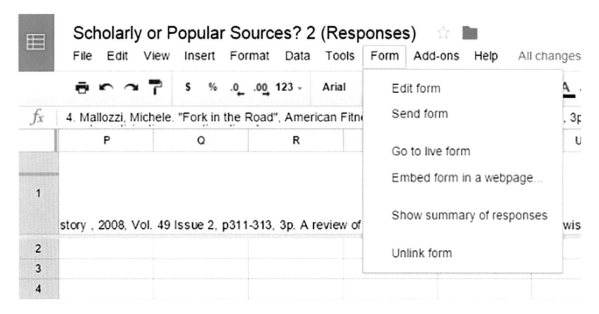

There are several Form tools which can be accessed from the destination spreadsheet. To access these options, go to the top toolbar of the spreadsheet and click on FORM, as shown above.

Both the *edit form* and *send form* options open the Form editing area. The *send form* option opens the dialog box for sharing the Form through email, etc.

The *go to live form* option opens the live Form that is completed by respondents. The *embed form in a webpage* option opens the *send form* dialog box in the Form editing area, which displays HTML code to be copied and pasted into blogs, wikis, online teaching environments and Webpages. Embedding a Form is a very effective way to share a Form with others, because it can be completed and submitted directly from the environment in which they are working. If you would like to embed a Form into another environment, such as a blog or wiki, check the *help* area of that tool for instructions on embedding.

Show summary of responses displays the visual graphic of the responses discussed earlier in this book, and the *unlink form* option unlinks a Form from the destination spreadsheet so that the Form can be used with a new spreadsheet for separate response gathering.

Chapter 8: Creating an Auto-Grading Forms Quiz

One of the most popular uses for Google Forms in the classroom is as an online assessment, such as a quiz or test. In the past, teachers either had to manually grade student responses from the response spreadsheet, or they needed to use a grading add-on, like *Flubaroo,* to grade student responses. *Flubaroo* is a wonderful add-on tool that automatically grades the student responses in the destination spreadsheet. It has many powerful features that will be discussed in Chapter 9 of this book.

It was announced in 2016 that Google Forms would have its own grading option and would no longer need the addition of an add-on to complete automatic grading. If you use *Flubaroo*, you might still want to keep it as an option because the Google Forms grading option may not do everything you want it to do - *yet.*

The Forms grading option does not grade a range of mathematical answers, while *Flubaroo* does not share a median quiz grade or a list of the most missed questions.

Both the Forms grading option and *Flubaroo* might suit a teacher's assessment needs, based on the type of feedback needed or the type of questions asked, so keeping both as grading option is a good idea.

The New Forms Quiz Option

Creating an auto-grading quiz in Forms is fairly easy. First, create the quiz and add the questions to the Form. **Google Forms can only auto-grade *multiple choice, drop-down,* or *checkbox* question types.**

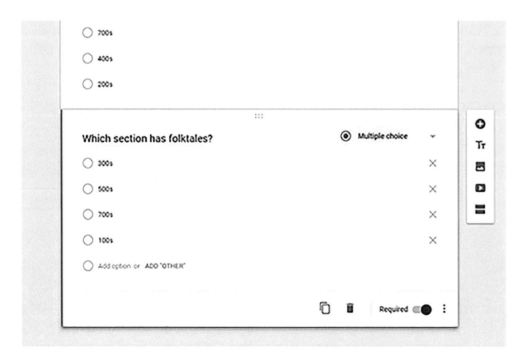

After the Form is created and the questions are added, open the (1.) *Settings* (gear icon) tab located at the top-right of the Form template. The *settings dialog box* will open.

Quiz Setting Options

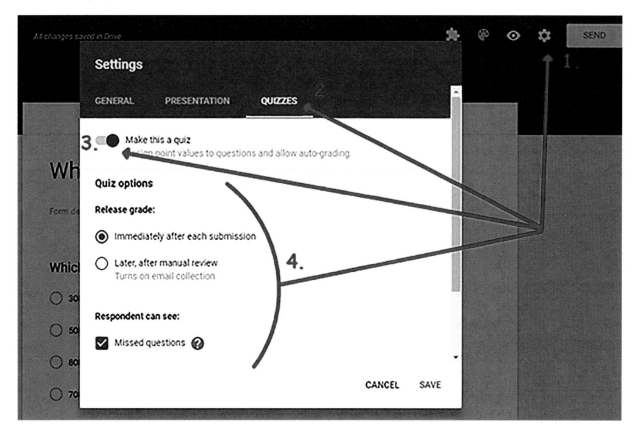

Click on the *Quizzes* tab (2.). The *quizzes options* will open.

Select the *Make This a Quiz* (3.) toggle. Additional quiz settings options (4.) will open when the toggle is selected.

If a quiz is being given to provide students with immediate feedback, the *release grade* option can be set for *Immediately After Each Submission.* Keep in mind that if this option is selected, students will basically receive the answer key that can be shared with other students who have not yet taken the quiz. Student will not receive immediate grade feedback if the *Later, After Manual Review* option is selected. Grade feedback will only be released by the teacher when the teacher chooses to do so. Email addresses MUST be collected for this option, because grade reports will be sent through email when the teacher releases them. This will be explained shortly.

If *Respondents Can See Missed Questions* is selected, students will see the incorrect responses as well as the correct ones when they view the graded quizzes.

Other quiz settings can be changed by selecting the *General* **(1.)** tab under *settings.* If a teacher has elected to manually release grades under the *quizzes* tab, the *collect email addresses* box **(2.)** will automatically check. Students will not receive a copy of their submissions unless the *Response Receipts* **(3.)** option is checked. The choices for sending response receipts include *if the respondent requests it* or *always.*

Students can be limited to one response **(4.)**, however this option requires a school to sign in to a Google account. As mentioned earlier in this book, the additional option for allowing students to *edit after submit* **(5.)** enables students to edit the contents of their Form and re-submit it, however the original response is also retained in the destination spreadsheet. The *See Summary Charts and Text Responses* **(6.)** enables the students to see a summary of every response submitted after the Form quiz is completed.

General Settings Options

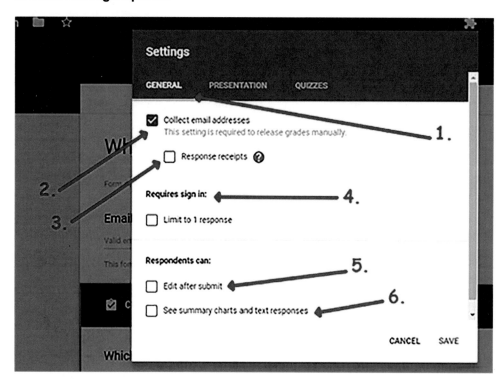

Once the quiz settings have been applied, and the creator returns to the quiz question editing area, a new option, *Answer Key,* will be available at the bottom of each question area.

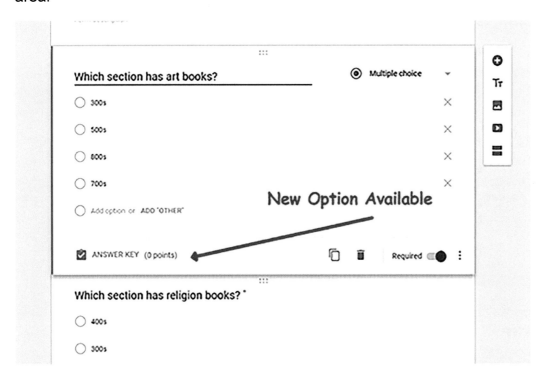

Click on the *Answer Key* link.

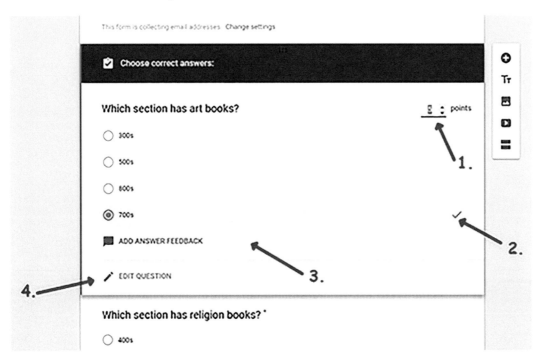

This screen enables setting the point value (1.) for a quiz, as well as designating the correct answer for the answer key (2.) Additional answer feedback (3.) can also be provided for students as well. This feedback can include online links to additional resources for question clarification or explanation.

If additional question editing is needed, or when the settings are completed on the answer key page, click *edit question* to return to the question editing page.

Viewing Responses and Releasing Grades

Once the quiz is completed, student responses will populate the Form (and destination spreadsheet if one is created) and grade summaries will be compiled on the *Responses* (1.) page of the Form.

Quiz Responses Page – Summary

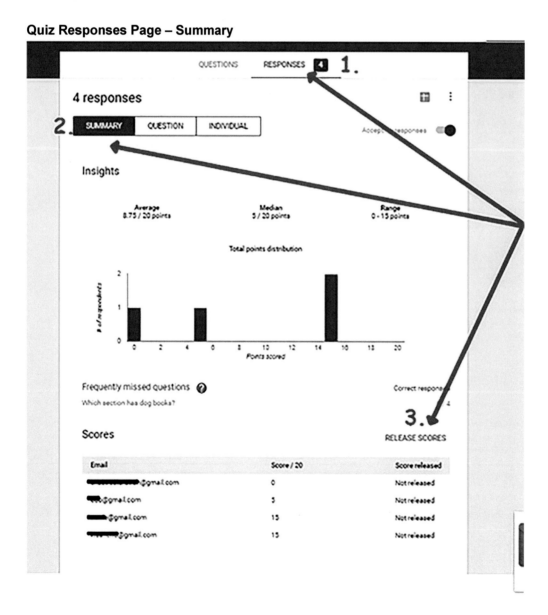

The quiz responses page has **three options** for viewing quiz and grading information. These options are: *Summary, Question*, and *Individual* and can be accessed by clicking on the designated tab (2.).

The *Summary* page is divided into two areas: *Insights* and *Scores,* as illustrated in the image above.

The *Insights* area displays the average, median, and range of points possible. It also displays the total point distribution in a bar graph and lists frequently missed questions.

Insights Area – Summary

| SUMMARY | QUESTION | INDIVIDUAL |

Accepting responses

Insights

| Average | Median | Range |
| 8.75 / 20 points | 5 / 20 points | 0 - 15 points |

Total points distribution

Frequently missed questions ?   Correct responses

Which section has dog books?   0 / 4

The *Scores* area displays each student's email address, the score the student earned, and the status of the grade release.

Scores Area – Summary

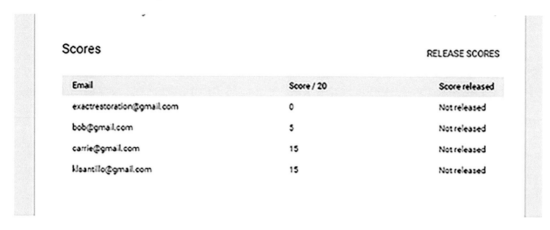

The *Release Scores* link opens another dialog box where all or individual students' grades can be selected for release. An optional feedback message can be included with the grade email. Check or uncheck the student email address, then click on *Send Emails and Release* to release grades.

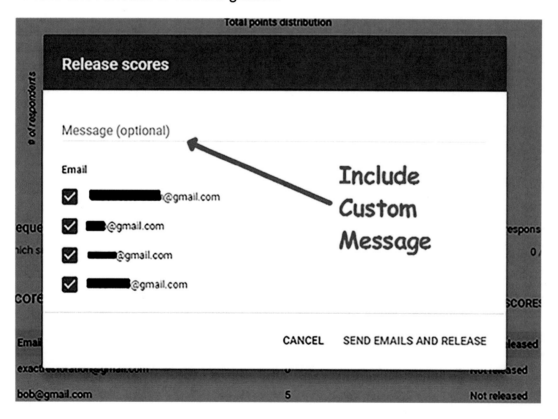

Once a student's grade is released, the student receives an email notification with a link to view the quiz results.

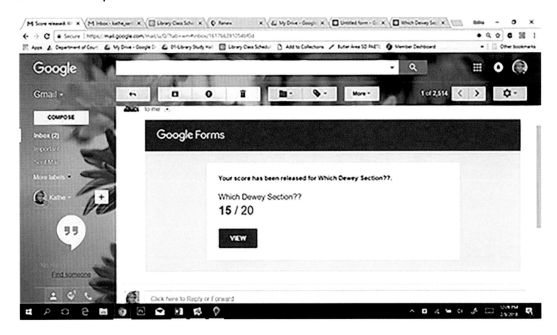

Student's View of Quiz Results

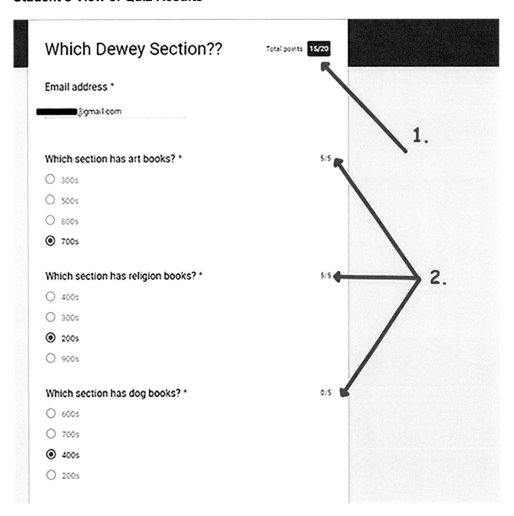

Students can see the total points earned **(1.)**; and the points earned earned for each question **(2.)**. If the quiz settings include sending response receipts, the student will see the correct response for any missed questions.

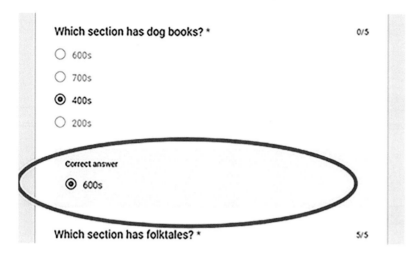

An *Item Analysis* is also displayed in the *Summary* area below the student scores. The *Item Analysis* illustrates how often each question was selected as an answer choice.

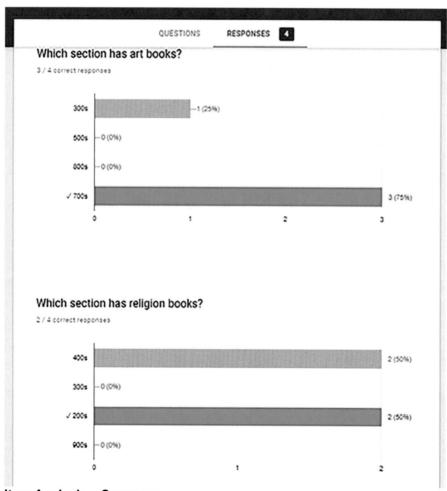

Item Analysis – Summary

The **Question** area of the *Responses* page displays the point tally for each question of the quiz.

Question Area

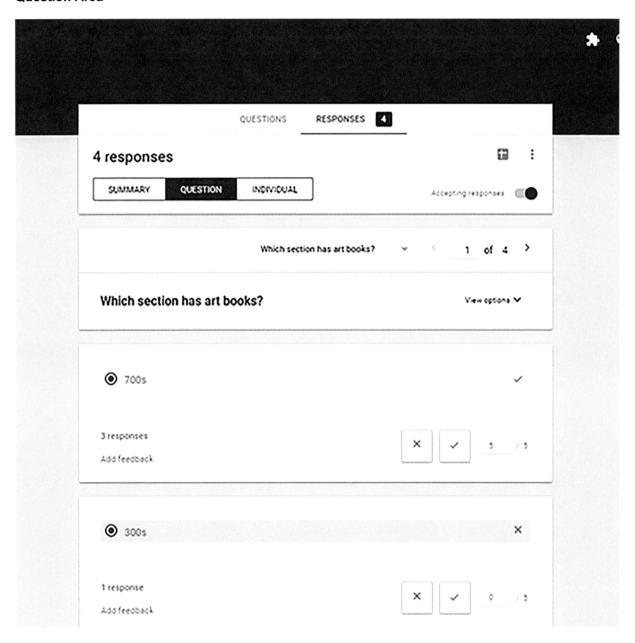

The *Individual* area shows each individual student quiz results. A *Release Grade* option, *Print* option, and *Delete* option are available at the top of each response.

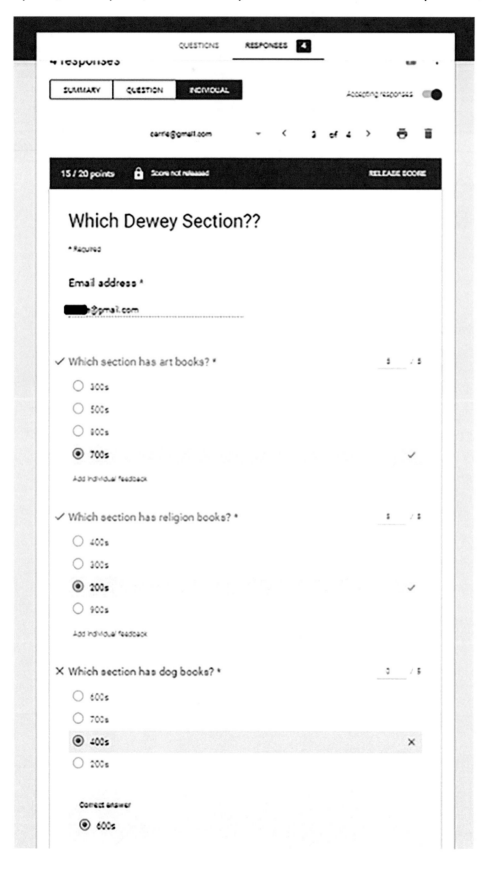

A *Destination Spreadsheet* can be created for the quiz Form as well, just as with any other Form type. Student scores will also be displayed in the Destination Spreadsheet.

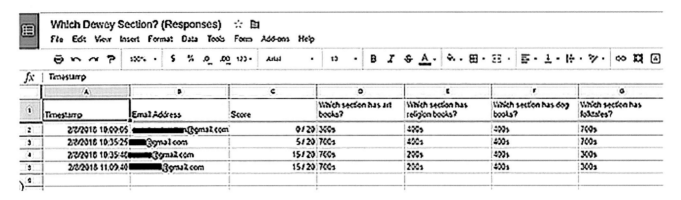

Chapter 9: Using *Add-ons* with a Destination Spreadsheet

Add-ons are small software applications created by third-party developers that can add additional functionality to your Forms and destination spreadsheets. Add-ons are installed to Forms/spreadsheets, and once installed, can be managed and turned on or off by the Form/spreadsheet creator.

To browse and install the add-ons available for Google Forms, click on the *Add-ons* option located in the top toolbar of the destination spreadsheet.

Flubaroo for Automatic Grading

Like conditional formatting, using an add-on, like *Flubaroo,* can aid in the assessment of Forms used for assignments, like quizzes and tests. *Flubaroo* is one of the many *add-ons* available to use with Google Forms.

Flubaroo computes average assignment scores; computes average score per question, and flags low-scoring questions for quick assessment; shows a grade distribution graph; gives the teacher the option to email each student their grade, and an answer key; and lets you send individualized feedback to each student.

Flubaroo is enabled through the destination spreadsheet. It must first be added using the *Add-ons* option in the top toolbar.

To add and use *Flubaroo,* follow the directions below:

1. Sign in to your Google Drive account, and open the Form to edit it.
2. Click on the *Responses* tab.
3. Click on the little green spreadsheet icon. The destination spreadsheet will open.
4. Click on *Add-Ons* in the spreadsheet toolbar, and select *Get add-ons...*

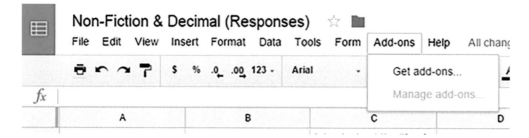

5. Type *Flubaroo* in the SEARCH ADD-ONS text box, and hit the ENTER key.

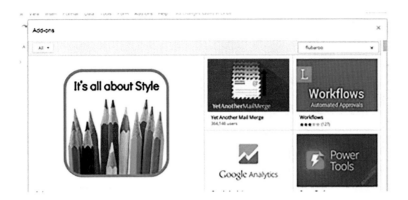

6. Click on the blue + *FREE* button to add *Flubaroo*.

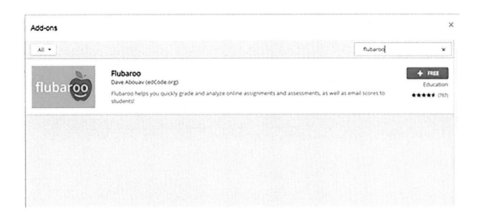

7. A dialog box will open. Read through the permissions and then scroll down and click on *ALLOW.*

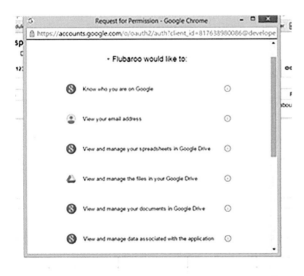

8. You will now have a message from *Flubaroo* in your spreadsheet that it is enabled.

Grading Responses with *Flubaroo*

Once students have submitted their responses, *Flubaroo* must be enabled in that spreadsheet in order to grade it. BEFORE using *Flubaroo* to grade the responses, you MUST also complete and submit a Form with the CORRECT answers selected to serve as the answer key for grading. It's a good idea to type ANSWER KEY in the name field to identify it in your spreadsheet later, as demonstrated in the image below. The answer key can be submitted before or after the student submissions, but make sure one is completed because *Flubaroo* needs it to grade the responses. I like to highlight mine answer key submission yellow so I know it's there.

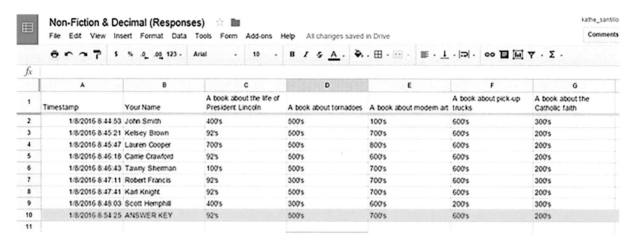

To enable *Flubaroo,* click on *Add-ons* in the spreadsheet toolbar. *Flubaroo* will be available in the drop-down menu. Hover the mouse over the *Flubaroo* option, and select *Grade Assignment.*

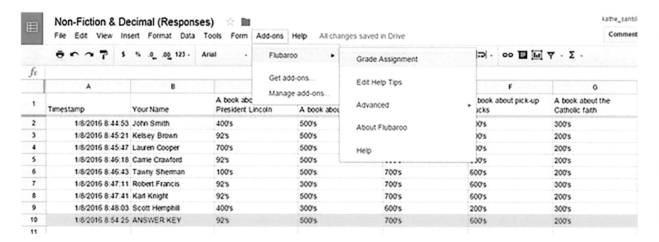

The first step opens in a dialog box. *Flubaroo* wants to know if it should grade the data in a specific field. You need to tell *Flubaroo* how each field is to be graded by using the drop-down menu to select it. For example, you would not want the name field graded, so you would select *Identifies Student* for it.

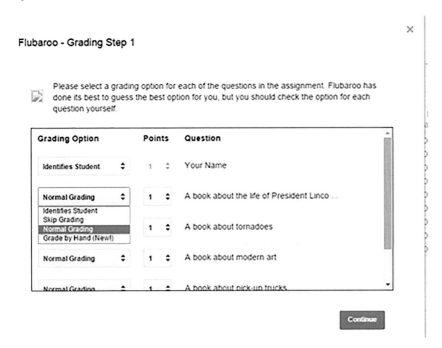

Click *Continue* when you have completed all of the fields.

Next, you need to tell *Flubaroo* which row contains the correct answers (the answer key you submitted). Click *Continue* when done.

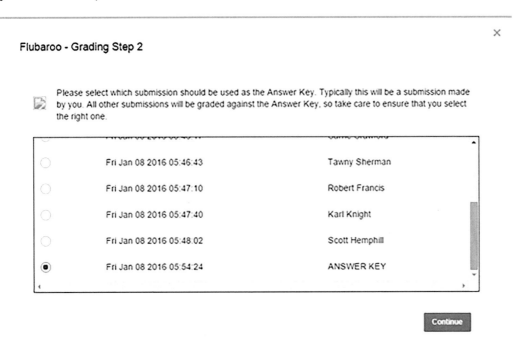

At this point, *Flubaroo* begins grading the responses, and opens a new sheet, called *Grades,* which contains the percentage correct/incorrect.

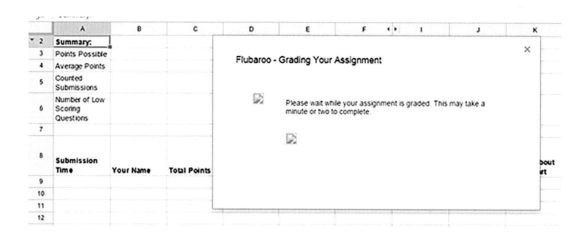

The *Grades* spreadsheet is separate from the original destination spreadsheet that houses the student responses. You can switch back and forth between the two spreadsheets by selecting the *Student Submissions* or *Grades* tabs at the bottom of the spreadsheet. The *Grades* spreadsheet will stay with the original spreadsheet so it can be referred to again later, if needed.

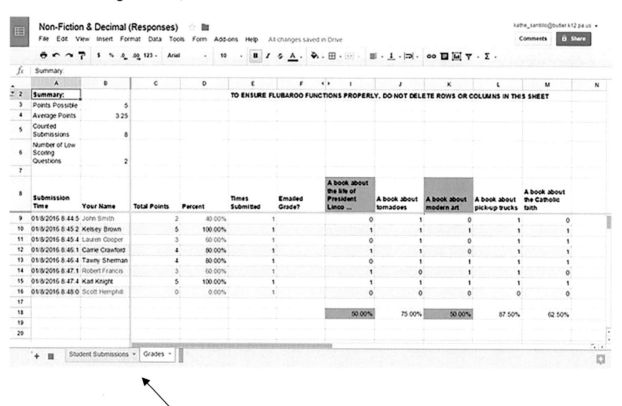

Spreadsheet Tabs

Flubaroo scores 1 point for a correct answer, and 0 points for an incorrect answer. It also shows which responses were not graded. If less than 60% of responding students got a specific answer correct, *Flubaroo* highlights the row in orange. Students who score less than 70% are highlighted by red text. These setting can be modified by going to *FLUBAROO* – ADVANCED – ADVANCED OPTIONS from the *Add-ons* option in the spreadsheet toolbar.

Printing Student Grades

Grade reports can be printed and distributed to students by clicking on ADD-ONS – FLUBAROO – ADVANCED – PRINT GRADES.

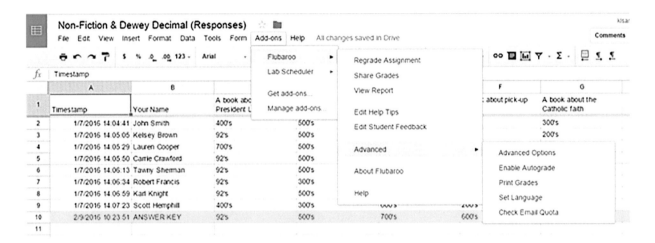

The *Print Grades* dialog box opens where option selections can be made and a personal message included. Click CONTINUE when done.

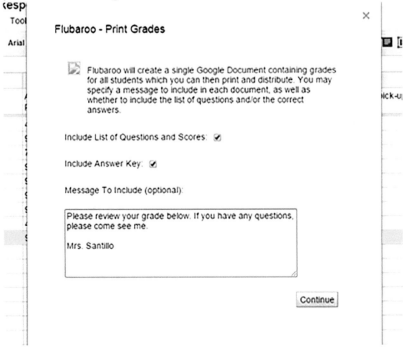

Flubaroo will generate a Google document (located in your Google Drive account) and include a link to it for printing or viewing.

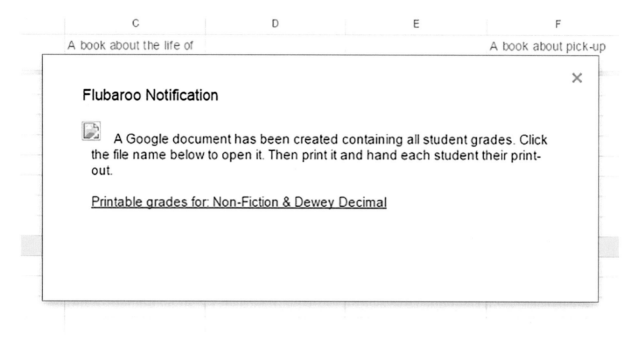

The printed report includes a separate page for each student with the student's score, each question listed, and the correct response (if *include answer key* was selected).

Non-Fiction & Dewey Decimal

Carrie Crawford
Thu Jan 07 2016 11:05:50 GMT-0800 (PST)
Your grade: 4 / 5 (80.00%)

Below is a message from your instructor, sent to the entire class
Please review your grade below. If you have any questions, please come see me.

Mrs. Santillo

Question	Your Answer	Correct Answer	Points
A book about the life of President Lincoln	92's	92's	1 / 1
A book about tornadoes	500's	500's	1 / 1
A book about modern art	600's	700's	0 / 1
A book about pick-up trucks	600's	600's	1 / 1
A book about the Catholic faith	200's	200's	1 / 1

Flubaroo Auto Grading

Flubaroo can also be set up to auto-grade submissions. When auto-grade is used, students receive a grade via email within minutes. Select ADD ONS – FLUBAROO – ADVANCED – ENABLE AUTOGRADE to use the auto-grading feature. Keep in mind, if students are submitting Form assessments at different times, you may not want to include an answer key with the emailed grades because it could be shared with others who have not yet taken the quiz or test.

Other *Flubaroo* Grading Options

Other options available in the *Flubaroo* add-on that are worth mentioning are:
- Add a sticker or badge to student grades
- The ability to grade multiple correct answers
- The ability to grade numerical ranges
- Grading of case sensitive answers
- Grading of extra credit questions
- Grading of partial credit for checkbox questions
- Grading questions by hand (*short text* and *paragraph* question types)

For more information about using the *Flubaroo* grading add-on, go to http://www.flubaroo.com.

Other Notable Add-ons

There are way too many add-ons to cover in this little book. The best way to learn about the add-ons is to browse the add-on store or to do a bit of online research to see what other teachers are using. And, like other software programs, the availability of the add-ons fluctuates when updates are made to the Google Forms tool. Some disappear, some appear. It's a good idea to periodically check what's available in the *add-ons* store.
Some add-ons are available through the destination spreadsheet toolbar, while others are available through the *more settings* menu in the Form editing area.

Here is a summary of some notable add-ons that are available at the time this book was written:

Save to Doc *(spreadsheet toolbar)* – This add-on takes the data in each row of the spreadsheet and converts it to a document in your Google Drive folder. This is a great add-on to archive quiz or test results to share individual student results with parents, administrators, etc.

Autocrat *(spreadsheet toolbar)* – This is a document merge tool. It combines and merges data from a sheet or form, and then create .pdf or Google Docs that can be shared through email or printed. *Autocrat* will be covered in the next chapter of this book.

Super Quiz *(spreadsheet toolbar)* – Another self-grading add-on. It's a little more involved than *Flubaroo.*

formLimiter *(Form toolbar)* – This add-on shuts off a Google Form after a specified maximum number of responses. This could be used with sign-up sheets for volunteers, field trips, etc.

Choice Eliminator *(Form toolbar)* – A great add-on for research topic lists, holiday party contributions, dates for parent conferences, etc. This add-on will eliminate an option from a *multiple choice, list,* or *checkbox* question after the respondent has submitted it. The selected option will no longer be available as a choice to subsequent students/parents.

Form Publisher *(Form toolbar)* – *Form Publisher* creates a Google Doc from a template and fills in the template with the Form responses. The Form/Docs are housed in a folder within your Google Drive account.

Chapter 10: Using the *Autocrat* Add-On for Document Merge

The add-on program, *Autocrat,* can merge data entered into a Form directly into a Google Drive document or Google Slide. These documents are saved to a specific Google Drive folder you create, and can be emailed as PDF attachments to students, parents, administrators, or other teachers. The documents can be created when the script is run or as soon as the respondent submits the Form. The steps for using *Autocrat* are:

> 1.) Create the Form.
> 2.) Create a template to receive the Form information when merged.
> 3.) Enable *Autocrat* on the destination spreadsheet and run the app to set up the merge.
> 4.) Run *Autocrat* on the spreadsheet either by enabling the auto-run *job triggers* in the set up or running it manually after all Forms are submitted.

Autocrat is a great tool to use if you prefer to have the ability to print professional-looking paper copies of Form assignments and assessments for parent/teacher conferences, etc. *Autocrat* can also be used to create professional development certificates and student awards through a Google Form, which can be automatically emailed to the recipient if the student or teacher provides an email address.

With *Autocrat,* information is entered here:

Goes to here:

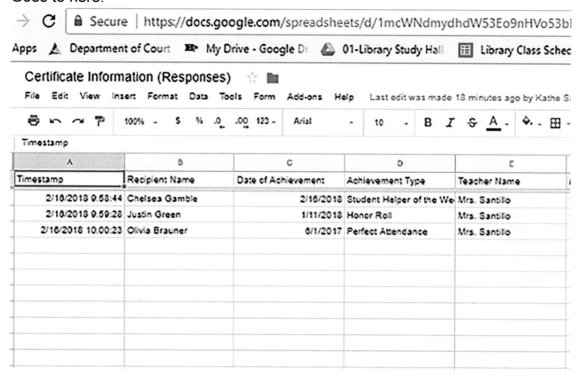

And becomes this:

Certificate Using a Google Slides Template

Google Forms does have a print feature to print individual responses directly from the Form *Responses* tab, but it may not look as professional or creative as you want. See the differences in the below illustrations:

Print-Out from Individual Response - Google Forms

Print-Out from Individual Response - Autocrat Document Merge

Setting up *Autocrat*

Autocrat is available through the spreadsheets add-ons menu. Open the destination spreadsheet, and select *Add-Ons* in the upper toolbar. Select *Get Add-Ons...* from the menu options.

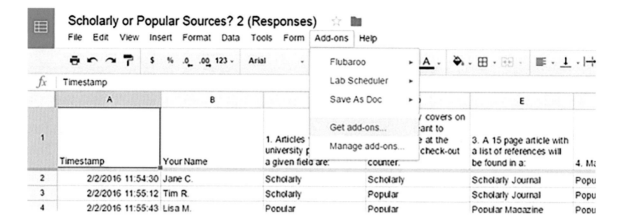

Type *Autocrat* in the search box of the add-ons store, and hit *Enter.* The app should appear in the list of results, as shown below. Click on the blue *+FREE* button to add it.

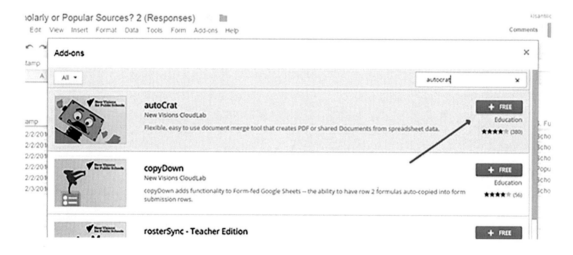

A *Permissions* dialog box will open listing all of the permissions the Autocrat software needs to your Google Drive account. Click *Allow* to continue.

Autocrat is now added as an option in the *Add-ons* menu of the spreadsheet.

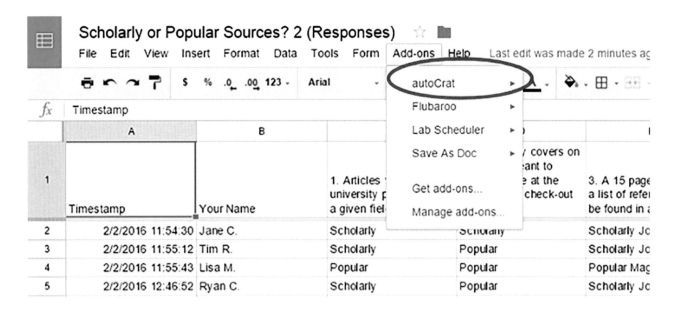

Once *Autocrat* is installed as an add-on, it is available on any spreadsheet, even though you may opt not to use it on all of them.

Enabling *Autocrat*

Before you can use *Autocrat*, you need to have a merge template. This is where the Form data will be sent. You can create the merge template before enabling *Autocrat,* or it can be created during the enabling process. I recommend creating the template *first,* which I'll explain here, then enable *Autocrat.* It's whatever you prefer.

Create the Merge Template

Open your Google Drive account. This is where you will create the folder and the merge template for the data in the Form. Click on the NEW button and select *Folder.* This example will be for a Form created to collect information for upcoming parent/teacher conferences.

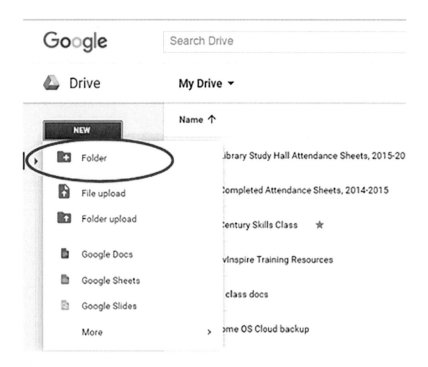

I prefer to create the folder first, and then open the folder to create the merge template. That way, everything is where it should be. Name the folder something that represents the contents. This helps to locate it easily later.

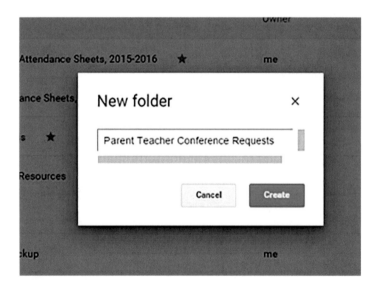

Double-click on the folder to open it. Once you are in the folder, click on the *New* button again, and select *Google Docs* this time. *Autocrat* also works with *Google Slides*, a part of the *Google Drive* suite. *Google Slides* is the better option when creating a certificate or award template.

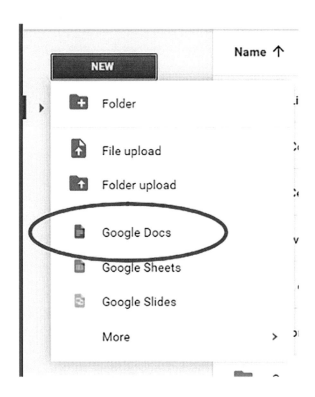

A blank, untitled document will open. You can create the document however you choose, just make sure to leave space for the *merge tags*. The merge tags designate where specific information from the Form/spreadsheet column will "fill in" the document.

The merge tags should represent the information that appears in the column headings found on the destination spreadsheet. They should be typed in the merge template by using two carrot << >> marks before and after the text that will be merged from the Form.

Column Headings

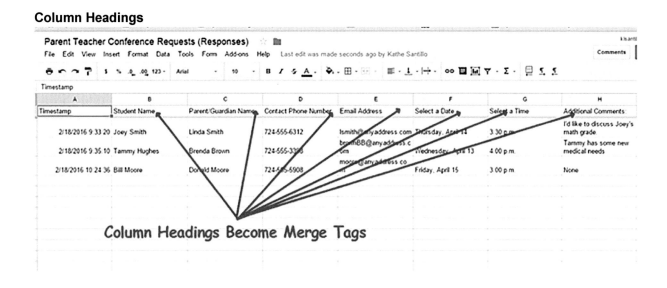

126

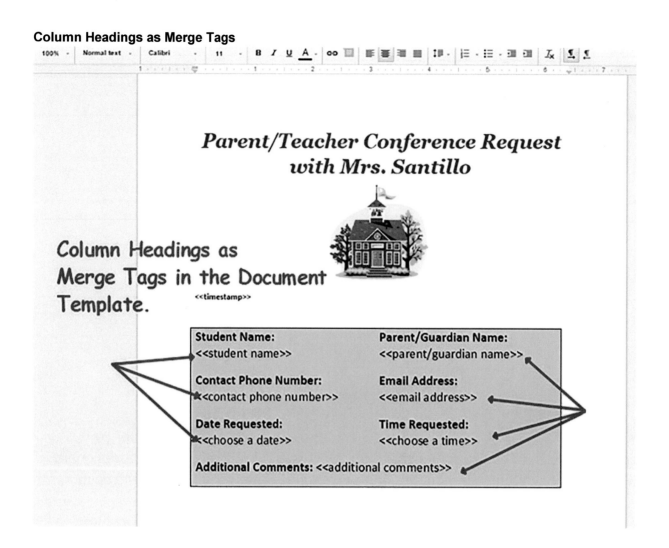

The merge tags do not have to be typed EXACTLY the same as the column headings, but they should be close enough that *Autocrat* recognizes which column of information feeds into that area.

Once the merge document has been created, return to the destination spreadsheet and select *Autocrat – Launch* from the *Add-Ons* dropdown menu. The image below shows it being set up after responses populated the spreadsheet, but it can be done prior to the Form being used/before the spreadsheet receives responses.

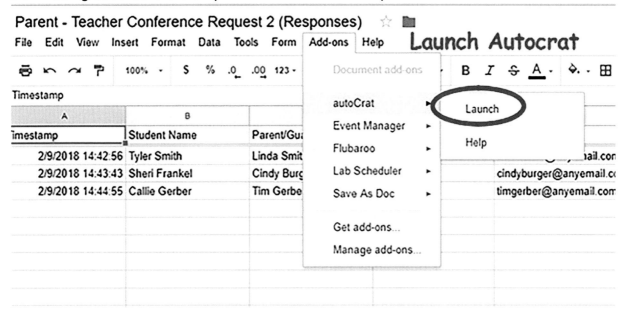

A dialog box will open. Click on the *New Job* button.

Another dialog box opens. Create a name for your merge job. Pick something that is easily recognizable for the job at hand. Click NEXT to proceed.

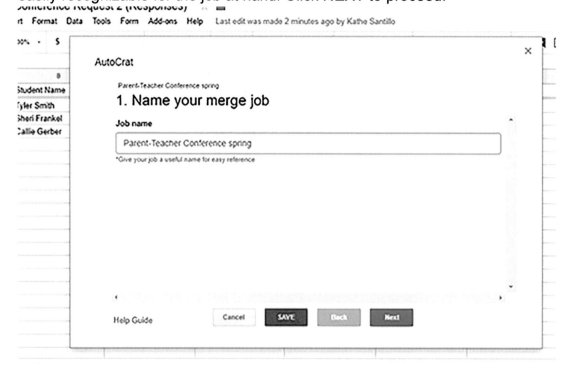

Next, you will be asked to locate the merge document template you created. Click on *From Drive* and locate the merge document. A template can be created here, but I recommend creating it earlier and finding it here. It's much easier to do it that way.

Once the merge template document is selected, document name will appear.

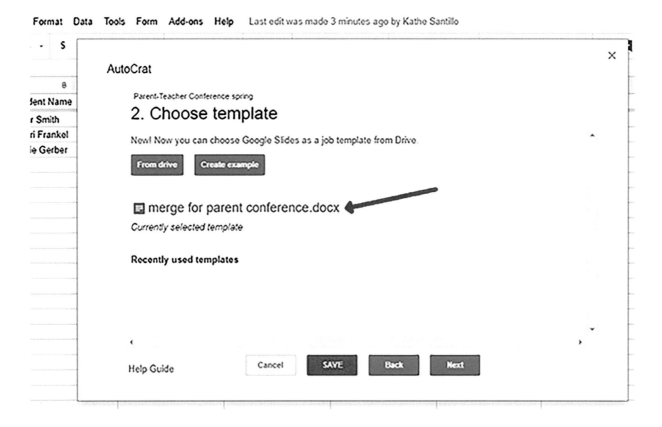

Click NEXT to proceed.

The next step tells *Autocrat* which information from the Form merges into which fields on the merge template document. Each field must be selected using the drop-down menu next to it. In the example below, the merge tag on the document for <<parent/guardian name>> will show the parent/guardian name from the Form, so that information is selected from the drop-down menu.

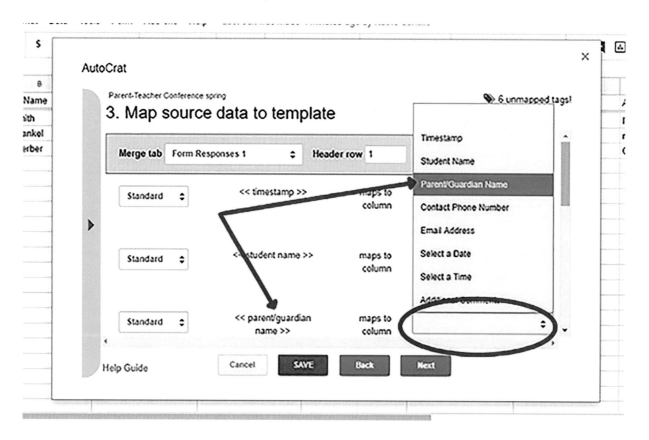

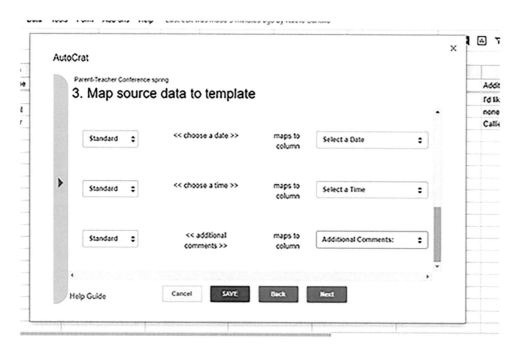

After you've verified that the correct merge tags match the correct information, click NEXT to continue.

Step 4 names the merged documents which will appear in your Google Drive folder once *Autocrat* is run and the documents are created. You can include one or more of the merge tags in the file name so that each document has a unique name. For example, in the document below, I'd like the student's name to appear after "parent-teacher conference". I can't simply type in the merge tag, <<student name>> after "parent-teacher conference". That won't work. In order for the student's name to appear so that each document has a unique name, I have to select and COPY the <<student name>> tag from a menu and PASTE it next to the document file name.

To do this, click on the light blue tab that is visible to open the merge tag names.

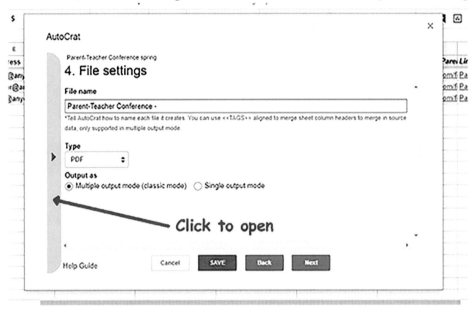

Click on the merge tag that you want to include in the file name. Clicking the tag copies it to the clipboard.

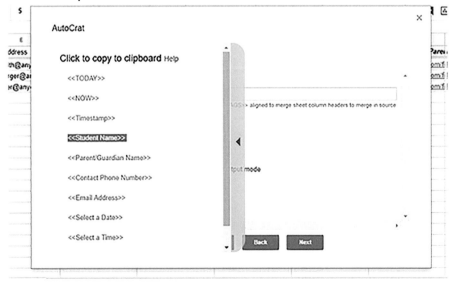

Close the light blue tab and click the cursor where the tag should appear in the file name box. Click Ctrl +V to paste the copied merge tag next to the file name. Now, each document will have a unique file name, such as "Parent-Teacher Conference-Callie Gerber; Parent-Teacher Conference-Tyler Smith", etc.

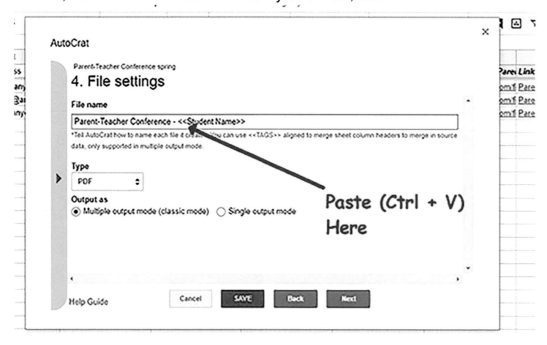

Click NEXT to proceed to Step 5. In Step 5, the destination folder is selected. This is the Google Drive folder where all the merged documents which are created from the Form go to once they are created. Select that folder, for example the *Parent Teacher Conferences* folder. If no folder is visible, select the blue *+Choose Folder* button to select a destination folder.

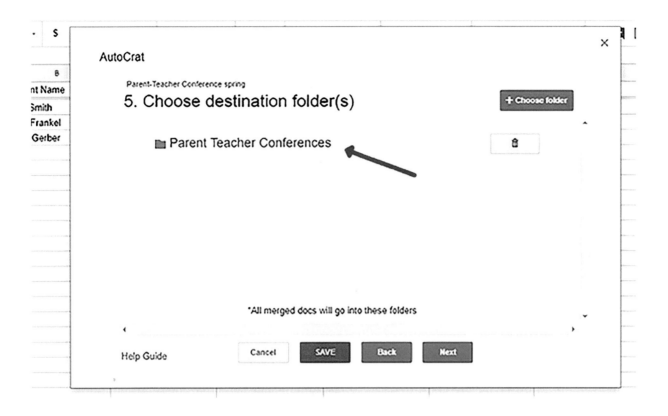

Most of the time, **Steps 6 & 7** for *Dynamic Folder* and *Set Merge Conditions* can be skipped. These options basically allow the document to be dropped in a different folder or only merge the document when certain conditions are met. Click NEXT to move through each of these steps.

Step 8 enables sharing the completed merge documents with the Form respondents. If the document is to be shared with respondents, make sure to include an email address on the Google Form the respondents complete, because the email address is pulled from the email address merge tag created earlier in the *Autocrat* set up.

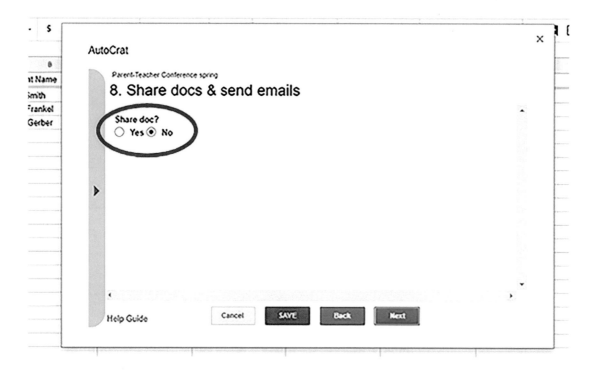

If the option is not to share the merged document, select *No* here and click NEXT to move on.

To share the document with the respondents, select *Yes.* Additional options will open.

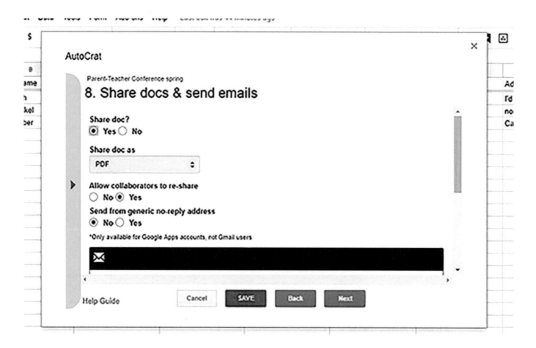

The merged document will be shared with the respondents as a PDF document.

Options are also listed to allow collaborators (those receiving the document through email) to re-share the merged document and an option to send from a generic no-reply email address. Check *Yes* or *No* for the share option and check *No* for the generic no-reply email address.

You must scroll this dialog box down to reveal a sample email header and body. In order for the respondents to receive the merged document via email, the email merge tag must be copied and pasted to the "To:" area of the email. Copy this merge tag the same way the <<student name>> tag was copied earlier by clicking on the light blue tab and clicking on the tag created for email addresses. In this example, <<email Addresses>> was used as the merge tag. Clicking on the tag copies it to the clipboard.

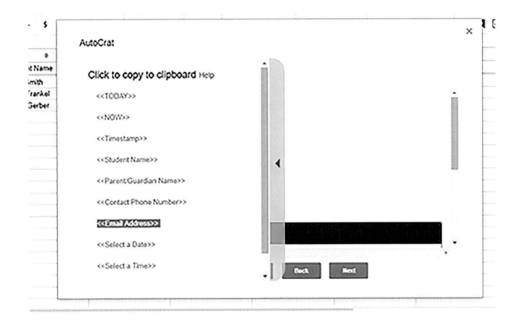

Close the light blue tab and click in the text box for "To:" and click Ctrl+V to paste the merge tag into the text box.

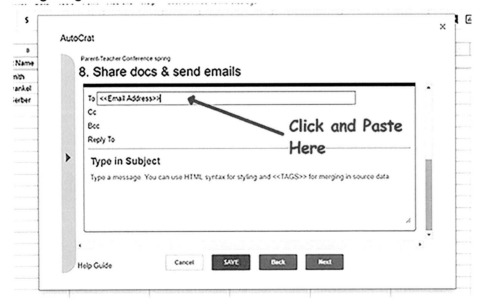

A message can be included in the email in the "Type in Subject" area.

Job triggers can be added in Step 9. A job trigger schedules when *Autocrat* will run on the destination spreadsheet and create the merged documents from the Form submissions. *Run on Form Trigger* runs *Autocrat* when the Form is submitted. If this option is selected, it's a good idea to also select an option for *Runs on Time Trigger* as well as a back-up.

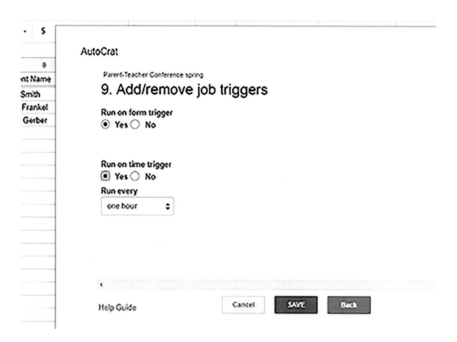

Click SAVE when the setup is completed and close the setup dialog box.

Running the *Autocrat* Merge

If Forms have already been submitted to the destination spreadsheet *Autocrat* can be run to create the merged documents for the responses already submitted.

Go to the *Add-Ons* tab of the destination spreadsheet and select *Autocrat – Open.*

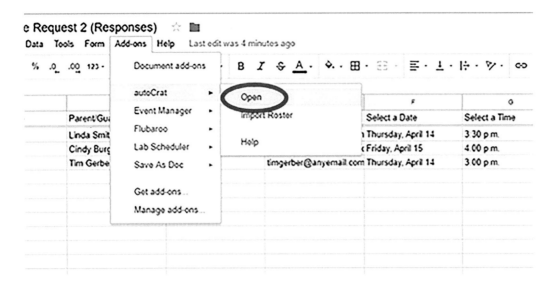

Select the *Run Job* button to begin running *Autocrat.*

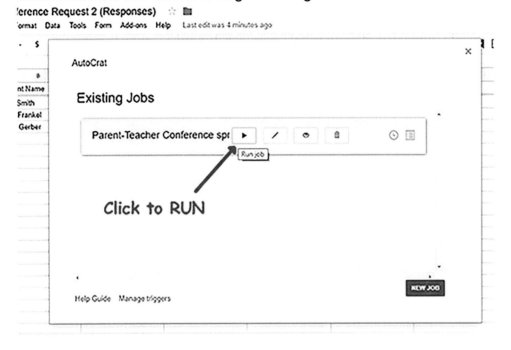

Click to RUN

When *Autocrat* has completed running, new columns of data will appear in the destination spreadsheet. .This includes a direct link to the merged document; a link that can be copied and pasted into correspondences; a document ID; and the time the merged document was created. Do not delete these columns.

The new, merged documents created by *Autocrat* are located in the Google Drive folder specified when the merge settings were completed.

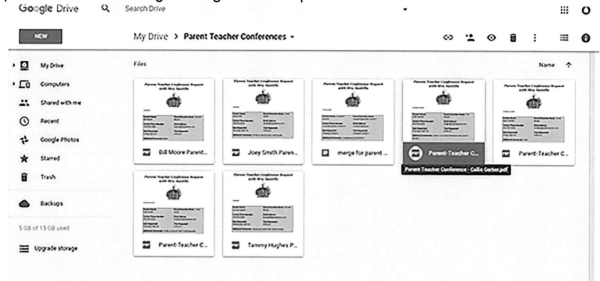

Below is an example of a completed merged document. If I had selected the document be emailed to specified recipients, this is also what they would receive, in PDF format.

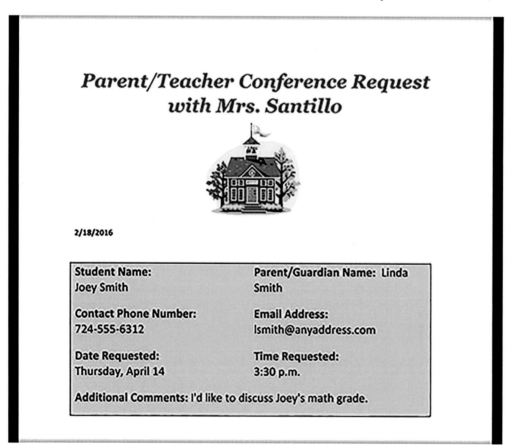

Autocrat can be used with any Form activity- quizzes, tests, reading journals, sign-up sheets, department meeting agenda submissions…..The possibilities are endless. Even though it make take a few minutes to set up in the beginning, *Autocrat* creates and shares professional looking documents from Form entries and streamlines data into creative or professional documents to share.

Autocrat includes many other powerful features to make your spreadsheet data really work for you, including a merge of data into *Google Slides*.

Go to http://cloudlab.newvisions.org/add-ons/autocrat for more information, or check out the many tutorial videos available on YouTube.

Chapter 11: Password Protecting a Form

Sometimes it is necessary to password protect a Form, especially if the Form is linked to or embedded on a class Web page, or if only certain people are required to complete it.

There is a way to password protect a Google Form. This can be done by creating a two-part Form using the *Add Section* option. Here's how:

1. Create a new Form, then click the *Add Section* to add a second section. You will use the first section as the password entry point.

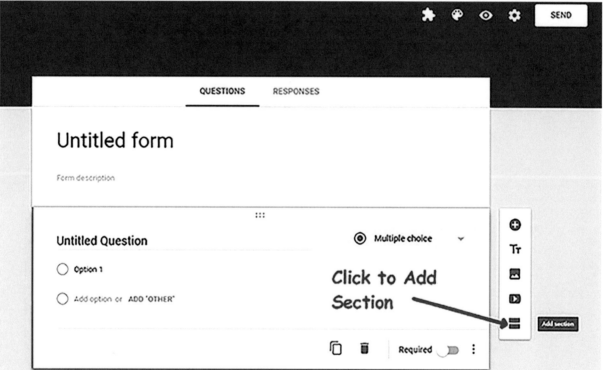

2. Name the first section of the Form the same as the second section (1.) Type in the password instructions in the *Untitled Question* field (2.) Change the question type to *short answer* (3.) and make the question a required one (4.)

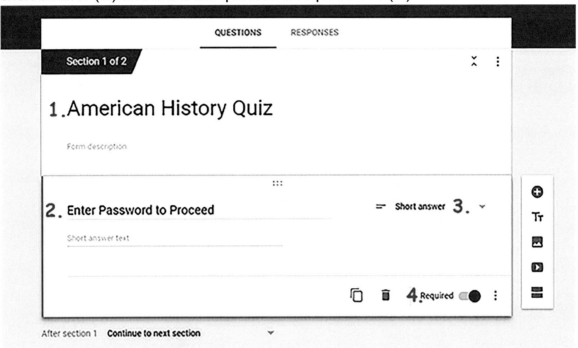

3. Next, click on the menu next to the *required* field and select *Response Validation.*

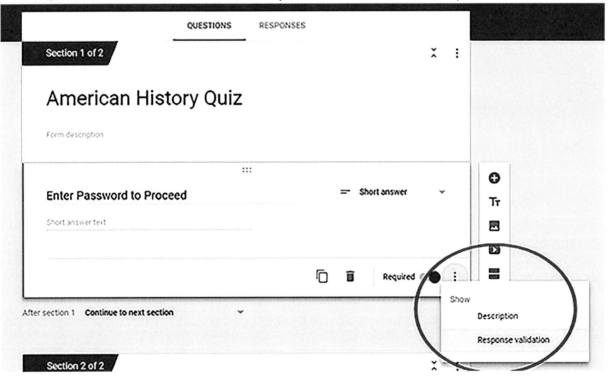

4. Change the drop-down menu options to "text" (1.) "contains" (2.) then enter the password you want to use in the *text* field. In this example, I'll use *tornado2018* as the password. You can enter custom text (4.) which the respondent will see if he/she enters the incorrect password.

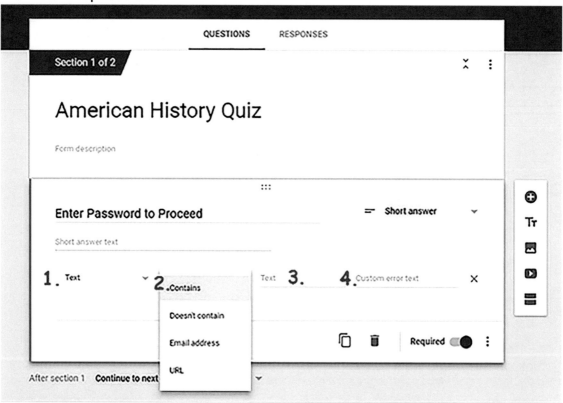

5. Now, move to the second section. Keep the option under section one set to *Continue to Next Section.* Click on the + button to add the first quiz question. Complete the rest of the Form as you would normally complete it.

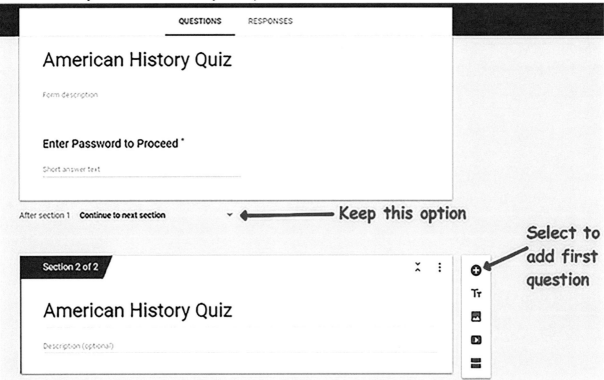

When students complete the Form, they will see the first section you created, but cannot proceed to the second section without entering the correct password.

Student View

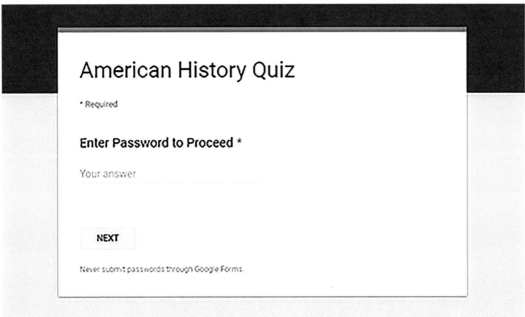

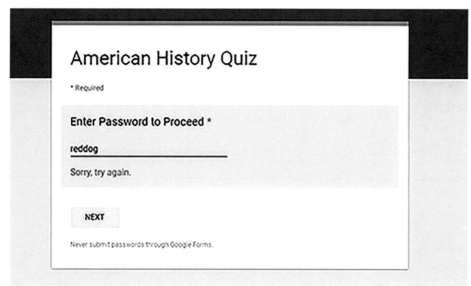

If the incorrect password is entered, respondents will NOT be able to view the rest of the Form. If the correct password is entered and the respondent clicks on NEXT, the rest of the Form will become visible.

Chapter 12: Guidelines & Suggestions for Classroom Management & Instructional Forms

At the beginning of this book, I provided a list of use examples for Google forms in the classroom (1.1 – Uses for Google Forms in the Classroom). The possibilities are endless for using Google Forms in the classroom. Basically, any document that can be created on paper can be created as a Google Form! Think about all of the paper documents currently in your file cabinet. Each one could be converted into a Google Form.

This chapter provides some basic guidelines and suggestions for creating some of the Forms on that list.

Parent or Student Sign-Up Sheets – Use *short answer* question types for short data fields, such as name, student's name, phone number. Make ALL fields required. This can be done in the individual Form, or set as a default for all Forms, which is explained later. Enable notification rules. If the sign-up sheet is being used for multiple events, the list of events could be added as *multiple choice* or *dropdown* question types. I recommend using the add-on, *Choice Eliminator*, which is available through the Form editing area, if parents or students are signing up for a task that has limited slots.

Class Information Management – This Form could be set up to collect contact information for parents, addresses, emergency numbers, etc. Use *short answer* question types for short data fields, such as name, student's name, phone number, address, etc. If a special instructions field is needed for something like medical information, behavioral issues, etc., use a *paragraph* question type. Make ALL fields required. Enable notification rules.

Make-Up Request Forms for Parents – Include *short answer* fields for the student information, such as dates work was missed, class period, student name, etc. *Paragraph* fields could be included for the longer assignment instructions.

Student Teacher/Colleague/Rubric Grading Observation – Observation forms and rubrics are perfect ways to use Google Forms because they can be used from a tablet and handheld device as the observation takes place. These types of Forms are ideal for incorporating the *linear scale* question type because it works so well with ratings.

Scheduling Parent/Teacher Conferences – Use the *short answer* fields for name, address, phone number, etc. *Paragraph* question types can be used for fields containing more information, like questions and concerns. All fields should be marked required. Enable notification rules to be monitor responses.

Lesson Plans – If your district does not subscribe to a service to house electronic lesson plans, Google Forms is a great way to archive them. Create the Form with *short answer* fields for the short data such as lesson name, and grade. *Dropdown* fields can be used for state standards, grade levels (if you teach multiple levels), and *paragraph* question types can be used for the detailed lesson information. I recommend using the add-on *Autocrat* or *Save as Doc* so that the lesson can be exported into a document and printed for substitute teachers or administrators.

Reading Record – Each time a student picks a new book, he/she can quickly enter the title and author in a Form. Use *short answer* question types. All student information can feed into one destination spreadsheet, which can be sorted by student name so that each student's reading record is available in one area of the sheet. It's a good idea to add a shortcut to the Form on classroom computer desktops so that students can access and complete it quickly.

In Conclusion...

There are so many ways to use Google Forms in the classroom. The best advice I can give you is to do a little Google searching to see how other educators are using this great tool. There is lots of information available online for creating and using Google Forms; many examples of Live Forms; and numerous video tutorials on YouTube and other sites which can guide you through creating and implementing Google Forms in YOUR classroom for assessment, instruction, and management.

Examples of Google Forms Uses

Parent-Teacher Conference Request

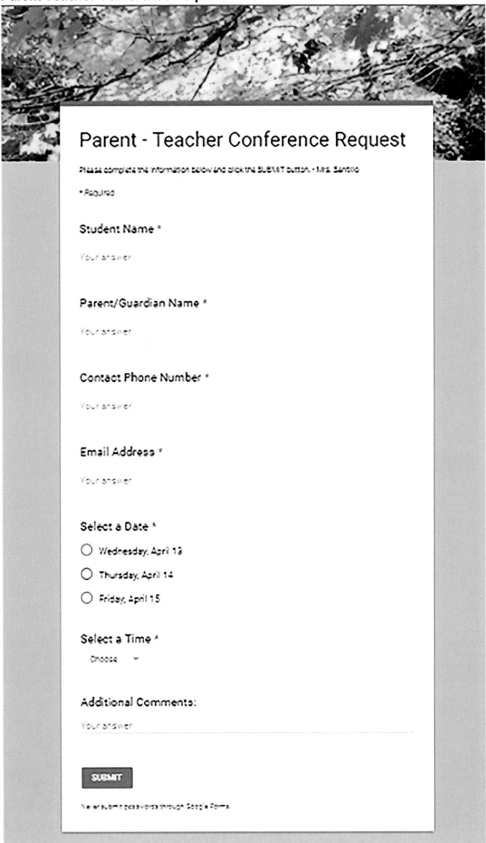

IR Reading Guide

* Required

Your Name: *

Your answer

Period *

Choose ▾

New Semester Book Title: *

Your answer

Author's Name: *

Your answer

Page Started: *

Your answer

Page Stopped: *

Your answer

Quarter #3; Guide #1: My Corrections

Look back on your Quarter #2 Guides. List two errors you repeated from the Quarter 1 Guides.
List 1 new error you noticed and highlighted.
Word each as statements that you will fix. They MUST be in complete sentences.

Error #1 you repeated from Quarter 1 *

Your answer

Error #2 you repeated from Quarter 1 *

Your answer

New error you noticed and highlighted: *

Your answer

SUBMIT

Public Speaking Rubric

* Required

The speaker made eye contact with the audience. *
Please rate the speaker's performance using the scale below.

	1	2	3	4	5	6	7	
Did Not Make Eye Contact	○	○	○	○	○	○	○	Made Eye Contact Throughout the Presentation

Rubric for Public Speaking
Please rate each speaker on his/her performance in each area.

	Excellent	Average	Fair	Poor
States the purpose.	○	○	○	○
Organizes the content.	○	○	○	○
Supports ideas.	○	○	○	○
Incorporates stories and examples.	○	○	○	○
Summarizes the main idea(s).	○	○	○	○

NEXT

Page 1 of 2

Possible iPad Apps

* Required

Name of App *

Your answer

Curriculum Areas of Application *
Select any that apply

☐ Math

☐ Social Studies

☐ ELA

☐ Science

☐ Reading

☐ Information Literacy/Study Skills/Study Management

☐ Foreign Language

☐ File Storage/Cloud Storage

☐ Other: _____

Brief Description of App Use *
Can copy and paste description from Website

Your answer

Cost *

☐ Free, full functions

☐ Free, limited functions

☐ Cost (list price in OTHER)

☐ Other:

Link to App

Your answer

Submitted By: *

Your answer

[SUBMIT]

Social Media Survey

Complete the questions below then click the SUBMIT button.

* Required

Do you have a Facebook, MySpace, Twitter, Pinterest, or Google+ account? *

○ Yes

○ No

Are your settings private or public? *

○ All Private

○ Most Settings are Private

○ Most Settings are Public

○ All Public

○ I don't have any accounts

Do you think that having your settings PRIVATE keeps others from seeing your photos? *

○ Yes

○ No

○ I don't have any accounts.

Have you ever tagged other friends in your photos? *

○ Yes

○ No

○ I don't have any accounts.

A. C.A.R.P. Website Checklist

Carefully read through and answer each question. Complete the checklist for EACH Website being evaluated. Click SUBMIT when done. - Mrs. Santillo

* Required

Team Names *
First and Last Names

Your answer

1. Title of Web Page or Site *

Your answer

Authority and Accuracy

2. Who is the author of the Website? *
If you find the author or organization name, choose OTHER, and type in the name.

○ I couldn't tell.

○ Other:

3. What authorship clues does the URL provide? *

☐ Company (.com)

☐ Academic Institution (.edu)

☐ U.S. Government Agency (.gov)

☐ U.S. Military Site (.mil)

☐ Network of Computers (.net)

☐ Non-Profit Organization (.org)

☐ Country-Specific Site (e.g., .uk)

☐ Personal Web Page (e.g., www.robertsmith.com)

☐ Other:

AUP Violations

* Required

Date of Occurrence *

Date

mm/dd/yyyy

Student Name *
(Last name, First name)

Your answer

Brief Description *

Your answer

Discipline Action *

○ Verbal Warning

○ Written Discipline Referral

○ None, student was already gone when infraction was caught

○ Other:

Additional Notes

Your answer

SUBMIT

Never submit passwords through Google Forms.

This content is neither created nor endorsed by Google. Report Abuse · Terms of Service · Additional Terms

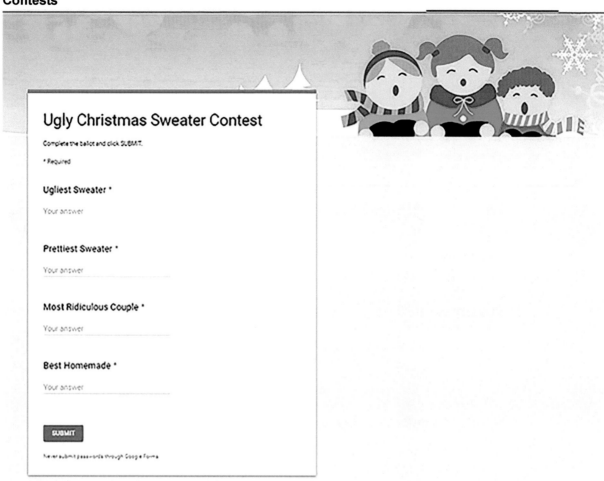

Ugly Christmas Sweater Contest

Complete the ballot and click SUBMIT.

* Required

Ugliest Sweater *

Your answer

Prettiest Sweater *

Your answer

Most Ridiculous Couple *

Your answer

Best Homemade *

Your answer

SUBMIT

Never submit passwords through Google Forms.

Instructional Mapping for SLO, 2016-2017

* Required

Date *

Date

mm/dd/yyyy

Teacher's Name *

Your answer

Class Periods *

☐ Period 1

☐ Period 2

☐ Period 3

☐ Period 4

☐ Period 5

☐ Period 6

☐ Period 7

☐ Period 8

Information Concepts Taught *

☐ Accessing, Identifying, and Evaluating Resources

☐ Behaving as a Digital Citizen

☐ Book & eReader Handling Skills

☐ Demonstrating Technology Etiquette & Safety

Made in the USA
Lexington, KY
25 April 2019